THE SWORDBEARER

John Knox and the European Reformation

Stewart Lamont

Hodder & Stoughton
LONDON SYDNEY AUCKLAND TORONTO

British Library Cataloguing in Publication Data
Lamont, Stewart
  The swordbearer: John Knox and the European Reformation.
  I. Title
  270.6092

  ISBN 0–340–55240–9

*Published by Hodder and Stoughton, a division of Hodder and Stoughton Ltd,
Mill Road, Dunton Green, Sevenoaks, Kent TN13 2YA. Editorial Office: 47
Bedford Square, London WC1B 3DP.*

Photoset by Medcalf Type Ltd, Bicester, Oxon.

Printed in Great Britain by Clays Ltd, St Ives plc.

Contents

Illustrations

Chronology

Introduction

The life story of John Knox is exciting enough in itself to warrant a new book. His influential role in Scottish and European history makes it even more important that his story be available to the general reader rather than made the preserve of scholars, devotees or detractors. Yet, considering Knox's importance, there are hardly any books in print about him. Tourists look in vain for explanatory material and cannot be expected to delve into libraries to learn the background to the momentous events which engulfed Scotland in the sixteenth century. It is partly to redress that balance that I have written this book, but it has also given me personal pleasure since many of the places mentioned in the story have touched my own life. Born within sight of Broughty Castle, where the ships which carried Knox to exile sheltered, I went to university in St Andrews, where many of the events described in the book took place. I lived for twelve years in Edinburgh and got to know the vennels and closes off the historic Royal Mile where Knox ended his days; and in my capacity as a broadcaster and writer on religious affairs have attended a score of meetings of the General Assembly, the pillar of democracy that he founded in Scotland. As a minister of the Church of Scotland I appreciate how much it owes to John Knox, and as a Scotsman I see how much he owed his psyche and temperament to his nationality and roots. The book was written in France, in the region that still displays Protestant heritage, and I hope it gives a perspective that is objective, but sympathetic.

Where quotations are used I have tried to simplify the spelling, although some of the Scots expressions do not strictly have an English equivalent. The bibliography is abridged since many of the books can only be found in specialist libraries. For the illustrations, I am most grateful to Roy Petrie of the *Glasgow Herald* for designing the chart of the Royal Houses of France, England and Scotland, and the map of Scotland; also to the National Library of Scotland for generous help with archive pictures for the illustration section. I take the blame myself for the photographs of St Andrews and Edinburgh. I would like to acknowledge my appreciation of the encouragement of the Hope Trust who made an advance order before seeing the completed work. In addition I would like to thank my agent Andrew Hewson, who suggested the book; two church historians who have given me help and advice – my former classmate, Dr Ian Hazlett of Glasgow University, together with the former Moderator, the Very Revd Dr Duncan Shaw; Johnston McKay of BBC Scotland; and Harry Reid, Deputy Editor of the *Glasgow Herald*, with whom I regularly work in my role as a freelance journalist.

Caylus, France
May 1 1991

MAP OF SCOTLAND
IN THE TIME OF JOHN KNOX

Moray Firth

ABERDEEN ○

DUNKELD ●   MONTROSE ●

T A Y S I D E   Firth of Tay

DUNDEE ○● ● BROUGHTY FERRY
PERTH ○● ● SCONE
CUPAR ● ○ ST. ANDREWS
FALKLAND ●

STIRLING ○   F I F E

Firth of Forth

LINLITHGOW ●   LEITH
EDINBURGH ○ ⊠ ● PINKIE ● HADDINGTON
GLASGOW ○ ● HAMILTON   L O T H I A N

BERWICK UPON TWEED

A Y R S H I R E

M A R C H E S

SOLWAY MOSS ⊠

E N G L A N D

Solway Firth

© Glasgow Herald

1

Prophecy Fulfilled

As the summer sun disappeared on the evening of Saturday,
June 10 1559 the town of St Andrews was unusually tense.
Outwardly there was no sign of the battle that was about to
begin. The grey stone buildings that clustered around the
cathedral had absorbed the two opposing forces assembled in
the town, which was the focus of the religious passions that were
about to be spent. The Primate of Scotland, Archbishop James
Hamilton, had only just arrived with a force of 100 spearmen
to try to head off the insurrection that was threatened, and had
issued a grim warning. If John Knox attempted to preach the
following morning at Holy Trinity, the parish church in the
centre of the town, the shots from a dozen hagbuts would land
on his nose.

Since his return to Scotland a few weeks previously Knox's
preaching had been having startling results. In his wake was
a trail of smashed religious relics, symbols of the old order and
of the religion he was determined to overthrow. It was likely
that a similar wave of iconoclasm would be triggered by his
sermon in St Andrews, and the Archbishop knew that his
cathedral and the priory that stood in its shadow would be among
the first targets. He also knew that the Prior of St Andrews
would be unlikely to stand in the way of the destruction. The
Prior, Lord James Stewart, was an illegitimate son of James V
of Scotland, but he was also one of the leaders of the Protestant
army which had plunged Scotland into civil war, and was there
in St Andrews as Knox's protector. Only a few weeks earlier

the Protestant revolutionaries could have been crushed at Perth
by the Queen Regent and the nobles. Now some of the nobles
had joined the Congregation, as the rebels called themselves,
and had brought the fight right into the headquarters of the
Catholic Church in Scotland. Knox knew that this was a make
or break moment for the movement.

It took considerable courage for Knox to mount those pulpit
steps, and some of his allies attempted to dissuade him from
doing so. But that pulpit was very special to Knox. From it,
a decade earlier, he had preached his first sermon in an equally
tense and violent atmosphere. He had longed for this moment
during his exile and had even had a vision of it as he lay ill in
the galleys within sight of the spires of St Andrews. Knox seized
his opportunity and presented himself at the church. The
Archbishop's soldiers did not move in for the kill and he made
the most of his chance. Taking as his theme Christ's ejection
of the traders from the temple in Jerusalem, there could be no
doubt about the signal he was sending to the congregation. They
went straight out of the church and destroyed the priory and
monasteries in the town.

From that moment Knox's legend was secure. We have
accounts of his preaching style which describe how he would
thump the pulpit and thunder his message with frightening
intensity. His actual sermon does not survive, but he is certain
to have made full use of the confrontational aspects of the
incident in the Bible and the text 'My house is the house of
prayer: but ye have made it a den of thieves' (Luke 19:46). The
pulpit he preached from is now situated in the university chapel
a hundred yards north of the spot and has been replaced by
a heavy marble one in Holy Trinity church. But we cannot fully
imagine the scene unless we have a picture in our mind of the
preacher himself – dark, brooding and intense. Although there
is much confusion about which portrait of Knox is the correct
one (see Appendix), there is a contemporary description which
helps us to imagine the scene on that day in 1559. This describes
him as follows:

In bodily stature he was rather below the normal height. His
limbs were straight and well-proportioned; his shoulders

broad; his fingers somewhat long. His head was of medium size, with black hair; his appearance swarthy, yet not unpleasant. His countenance, which was grave and stern, though not harsh, bore a natural dignity and air of authority; in anger his very frown became imperious. Under a rather narrow forehead his eyebrows rose in a dense ridge; his cheeks were ruddy and somewhat full, so that it seemed as though his eyes receded into hollows. The eyes themselves were dark-blue, keen and animated. His face was somewhat long, with a long nose, a full mouth, and large lips of which the upper one was slightly the thicker. His beard was black, flecked with grey, thick and falling down a hand and a half long. [Dickinson, lxxxxvii]

The John Knox who appeared in the pulpit of the parish church of St Andrews that Sunday in June 1559 was a different man from the trembling figure who gave his first public sermon there ten years earlier. During that decade he had mixed with royalty and leading Reformation figures. He now had confidence as well as courage. He had experience of suffering and of life which gave an added authority to his preaching. Having spent most of the decade outside Scotland, he came with the breath of fresh ideas and a forthright way of expressing them that went down well with the congregation. Nor was the Knox of the summer of 1559 the man of ten years later, whose broken health and broken dreams were infected with bitterness. This was a man at the height of his powers. He did not reach that position of commanding influence by birthright, wealth or even scholastic achievement: the story of that decade is an adventure which includes assassinations, revolution, confrontations with monarchs and firebrand performances in the pulpit.

Compared with other leading figures in the Reformation, Knox was the one who, from the beginning, most deserved the title of man of action. If we examine the way in which the others made their debut we find Calvin writing a scholarly work at the age of twenty-three; Cranmer scanning his Bible to find texts which would justify his king divorcing his wife to marry his mistress; and Luther hammering his theses to a church door in Wittenberg. As Jasper Ridley observed, Knox is the only one who makes his first entrance carrying a two-handed sword. He did so as temporary bodyguard to a leading Protestant preacher and was soon to lay it aside, but the sword is a fitting emblem for a dramatic life which cut across France, England and Scotland and earned him a place of honour on Switzerland's monument to the Reformation in Geneva. Knox's mission would not have succeeded without violence and, unlike his fellow-Reformers in Europe, he advocated armed opposition to rulers who stood in the way of his ideals. His tongue and pen were themselves a two-handed sword with which he won his place in Scottish history – dominating its church and achieving for him the status of patriarch and prophet – the Ezekiel of Scotland.

Some historians have queried whether it was John Willock and not John Knox who was the brains behind the establishment of a Reformed Church in Scotland, since, if we put aside Knox's own version of events, contemporary sources have surprisingly little to say about him. The English ambassador said of Knox in the years immediately after 1560, 'He ruleth the roost'; but George Buchanan managed to recount the history of Scotland from 1560 to 1568 mentioning him only once, as the preacher at the coronation of James VI. Knox's own *History* is more of a set of memoirs – or as one writer put it 'a sermon without an audience, a preaching book, one long inflammatory speech on behalf of God's truth as he saw it' – and thus liable to reveal more about himself than his place in history.

The contradictions and complexities of the man are reason enough to warrant reconsideration of John Knox. Until now he has tended to attract the attention of writers who were either scholars, hero-worshippers or antagonists. Some have carried their Protestant piety to the point where both history and the individual have passed out of focus into mythology. Others have tried to debunk Knox as a bigot and have only succeeded in making their portrait of him a harsh and unnatural caricature. In the film *Mary Queen of Scots* one incident unintentionally strikes a comic note. Mary is riding through the countryside outside Edinburgh when, from behind a bush, out rushes a strange-looking man with a long black beard who begins to berate her. This, the makers of the film would have us believe, is John Knox. Although the four occasions on which the two figures actually met were at the Queen's behest, the image of John Knox as a cross between Ian Paisley and the Ayatollah Khomeini seems to have become firmly lodged in the popular mind, with the Scots Reformer perched in his pulpit like a black carrion-crow picking over the weak flesh of his listeners.

Yet behind the myth there is a more complicated story of a frustrated man who enjoyed brief successes during a life of fifty-seven years. He might easily never have returned to Scotland, had not his passionate outburst against the English Queen Mary alienated her successor Elizabeth. That legacy and his sour relations with the much-romanticised Queen of Scots made it easy to portray him as oppressive in his attitude to women, whereas the passionate prophet had tender relationships with a number of women, which have either been eclipsed by the myth or used by his detractors to portray him as a Bluebeard. Far from ruling Scotland like an Ayatollah, Knox spent more than the first half of his life in humble obscurity, and more than half of the second in Europe. After his return to Scotland in 1559 his role at centre-stage was to last only six years, and in 1572 he died, burnt-out and embittered at the way his revolution had been thwarted.

More recently there have been those who have tried to mine the seam of Knox's writings to extract an ideology. As Marxism has been distilled from Marx, so they have tried to isolate Knoxism from Knox; but they have inevitably been frustrated because Knox was a man of action rather than a thinker. He was not in the same league as Calvin as a scholar of Scripture and he pales beside Luther as a theologian. But his preaching and writing were passionate and dynamic and had tremendous contemporary force, though not many of his sermons survive in print. As well as pamphlets and the four books of the *History of the Reformation* (volume V is generally thought to have been compiled from his notes), many of Knox's personal letters survive and these provide an inner dimension to his character which enables him to be fully understood. The passion of Knox's performance is inseparable from its success, and much of that flowed from the personality of the man.

Knox combined charisma with a cause. It so happened that

the moment had arrived for Scotland to embrace the cause of protestantism and it was Knox's fate to be instrumental in making the Protestant revolution happen. He undoubtedly derived much of his dynamism from injustices which existed at the time and a widespread appetite to replace the old ways by the new. Knox could find plenty of ammunition in the resentment felt by the people about the decadence and abuse of the sixteenth-century church. The nobility was not yet willing to loosen its grip on power and there was insufficient support from the emerging merchant classes for redistributing wealth or power. Even Calvin and Luther were not willing to challenge 'the powers that be who are ordained of God'. Knox went much further than the European Reformers in advocating the duty of a people to rebel against unjust and wicked monarchs. Sixteenth-century Scotland was ripe for the Reformation but not yet for the scale of revolution that convulsed Europe in later centuries.

In the sixteenth century the chess game of politics was still played between popes and emperors, kings and queens. It was rarely decided by the pawns, into whose ranks Knox was born and raised. Knox was less concerned with political power than with filling the role of prophet in its Old Testament sense. His vision of a proto-welfare state in the *First Book of Discipline* would have provided education for all and a more democratic society. It conflicted directly with the designs of the nobility, who were only intent on carving up the Roman Church's patrimony, and Knox was inevitably destined to be swept aside. He was too radical for them, and in that respect not only out of tune with his time, but ahead of it.

The freedom fighters and liberation movements of the twentieth century are more in tune with Knox's ideas than he was with the humanist intellectuals of the sixteenth century. However, if we look for parallels between Knox and revolutionaries of our own time, we will not find his equivalent among the Hitlers, Lenins or Maos whose primary aim was to seize and control political power. His support of violent struggle makes it difficult to equate him with religious leaders like Martin Luther King or Mahatma Gandhi. Nor did Knox possess the kind of religious personality which bids to control a whole nation, such as that of the Ayatollah Khomeini. In any case it is doubtful if the nation would have accepted him as leader, even if there had been universal democracy in Scotland, since the initial strength of the Protestant 'tribe' has sometimes been overestimated [Lynch]. Knox was a tribune of the people rather than a new Caesar. Despite the affection he acquired for English and Swiss ways, he was born and brought up a Scot and as such always possessed the mentality of the citizen of a small nation, one which is prouder of its poets than its princes. Knox's mindset is that of a rebel. It is no coincidence that many of those who assembled in the eighteenth century to sign the American Declaration of Independence came from the same ecclesiastical heritage as Knox.

However any parallel we might seek in our own century would inevitably be a false one. The nature of relations between church and state in the sixteenth century and the common assumptions about the rights of rulers over their subjects made it inevitable that a religious reformer could not avoid being a political animal. If he had lived today Knox would have been a political figure as well as an ecclesiastical one, and perhaps the closest parallel would be found with the liberation movements of Africa or Latin America. But embracing the principles which were dear to Knox in today's world is a very different matter from doing so in the mid-sixteenth century. What will emerge from these pages is not another Ian Paisley, although much of the Belfast preacher's earthy humour and barnstorming oratory might be reminiscent of Knox; Paisley's theology and his opponents, is as behind his times as Knox's was ahead of his own.

Knox does not enjoy universal admiration in his own country. He is a much-neglected figure when compared with Scotland's national poet Robert Burns, who had many more character flaws than Knox and made less of a contribution to the history of Scotland. It is easy to understand why poets make better romantic heroes than preachers, but the lack of tourist material on Knox and the paucity of popular material in print about him betray the fact that many of his fellow-countrymen do not regard him as a hero. For instance, his grave is now a car-park space for lawyers, and the pulpit and church where he preached have nothing to remind visitors of the momentous events which occurred in them. This cannot be explained entirely by ignorance or apathy. Nearly everyone knows who John Knox was. The problem is more that the myth of a tyrannical Calvinist has taken over and such a figure today is rejected rather than admired. Hopefully this book will supply enough information about Knox to enable readers to draw their own conclusions about someone whose place in European history is recognised in a monument in Geneva but who still remains a shadow in his own country.

The facts of Knox's life are well known and enough survives of his own writing to enable us to form an impression of his character and personality. But of the influences which shaped that personality we know little. Knox's own voluminous history of the Reformation in Scotland, in which he figures largely (often in the third person), is silent about his early years. It is not surprising that someone who inveighed against the corruption and false basis of the Roman Catholic Church would in hindsight want to play down the period when, as an ordained priest, he was himself part of its organisation. Knox is silent about many details of his life and it was only when the quatercentenary of his birth was about to be celebrated in 1905 that it emerged that he was probably born a decade later than 1505. The celebrations none the less went ahead though Hay Fleming's case for Knox being born in 1514 is now generally accepted (see Appendix).

Beza puts his birthplace as Gifford, a village near Haddington in East Lothian, but it did not exist as a town under that name at the time and is more likely to have been the Giffordgate in Haddington. The entrances to Scottish towns were often given the name gate or 'gait', referring to the direction in which they led – in this case the road to the Gifford estate. Haddington was known as the Lamp of Lothian and had three chapels, two monasteries, an abbey and three churches, one of which, St Mary's, is now the centre of an ecumenical pilgrimage in which the passions of the sixteenth century are exorcised.

His parents are unlikely to have been high on the social scale (approving biographers such as Buchanan could only find cousins in the west who were gentlemen). Knox states that he told the Earl of Bothwell in 1564 that his father, grandfather and great-grandfather had served his predecessors and 'some of them have died under their standards'. The Bothwells were the power in the land around Haddington and Knox's family may well have rallied to their standard before the battle of Flodden in 1513, answering the call for all men between sixteen and sixty to fight the 'ancient enemies of England'. The manner of the expression suggests a battle royal rather than a skirmish and there were no major battles for fifty years prior to Flodden. If Knox's father died in the huge casualties at Flodden, it would explain no further mention of him and would put the latest birth date for John Knox as spring 1514. Knox had a brother William who became a merchant in Prestonpans and a Protestant in middle life. It was common for Scots names to be written in any number of variant spellings and some omit the K and refer to him as Nox, near enough to the Latin words for night and a criminal (*noceus*) for his enemies to jibe '*quasi nox, a nocendo*' (or, like darkness from the doing of dirty deeds).

His mother's maiden name was Sinclair, and he used the code-name John Sinclair when writing to Scots Protestants in Edinburgh after 1555, since his own name would probably have resulted in the letter being seized. The fact that there are no further references to Knox's mother have led some to suggest that she also died early in his life. He acted as notary some years later for James Ker of Samuelston, a Lothian laird whose wife was a Sinclair and who was well connected to the Scottish nobility through his own family.

Whether or not he was a yeoman farmer, Knox's father seems to have been able to provide for his sons to be educated, since Knox went to university. Here again we meet conflicting evidence. Knox only mentions having attended St Andrews University, but the original 1505 birthdate combined with a mention of a John Knox at Glasgow University in 1522 has led some to say that Knox went both to Glasgow and St Andrews. Beza's statement that he studied 'at the feet of John Major' could confuse us still further, since Major was at Glasgow in 1522-3, St Andrews 1523-6 and returned there from Paris in 1531 to teach theology. If we accept 1514 as Knox's birthdate, it is clear that, even although men went to university in their early teens, he could not have been there at the age of eleven or twelve in 1525-6, and thus it was to St Andrews that he went after 1530, aged about sixteen. Haddington was part of the archdiocese of St Andrews and it would make more sense for him to have made the short sea crossing to Fife than to have attended either of Scotland's other two universities, Aberdeen and Glasgow.

There is no record of Knox graduating from St Andrews, where he would have completed studies in arts before moving to divinity. Records of Jesuits active in Scotland after the Reformation, which came to light this century, note that Knox was ordained a priest by the Bishop of Dunblane, William Chisholm, on Easter eve, April 1536. Buchanan refers to an ordination 'before the time ordinarily allowed by the canons' (that is, age twenty-four). This adds strength to the 1514 birthdate as well as raising the question why Knox applied for a dispensation. Perhaps the money was running out to pay for his studies and if he was an orphan he would want to start earning. The fact that he got the dispensation was not unusual, since in 1534 Pope Clement VII was showing no reluctance in granting them. James V of Scotland managed to appoint three of his illegitimate sons, all under five years of age, to be abbots and priors of the five richest monasteries. The fact that Knox's own archbishop (James Beaton, uncle of David, the future Cardinal) did not perform the ordination is not unusual. When we next pick up his trail he is acting as a notary in his native Lothian and signing himself 'Sir John Knox', the title which would have been used by a priest without a Masters degree. Those who bore it sometimes attracted the mocking description of 'pope's knights'.

It was no surprise that, owing to the vast surplus of priests in Scotland, combined with the siphoning-off of benefices, Knox could not find a parish. He would have lacked connections. But by turning his talents to the para-legal work of the notary apostolic he could earn more than a chaplain. Another course open to him was to act as private tutor to a wealthy family. Between 1540 and 1543 he apparently did both these things, acting several times for Ker of Samuelston and tutoring the family of William Brounfield. A notary deed of March 27 1543 bears the formula by which Knox describes himself 'minister of the sacred altar in the diocese of St Andrews, notary by apostolic authority' and refers to Paul III as Pope 'by divine providence'. The last extant notary document prepared by Knox is dated the following day and bears the addition, 'Witnessed in faith through Christ to whom be the glory', leading some scholars to conclude that by that date Knox had become a Protestant.

The spring of 1543 was the period when the Protestant cause blossomed briefly. Two of Arran's newly-appointed chaplains, Thomas Gwilliam, formerly Prior of the Blackfriars in Inverness, who was brought up not far from Haddington, and John Rough, a freelance preacher, were undertaking a preaching tour of Scotland and arrived in Lothian. Knox later reflected that he found Rough more 'vehement' against impiety and superstition, but it was the Lothian friar who is credited by the historian Calderwood as being 'the first man from whom Mr Knox received any taste of the truth'.

About the same time as his apparent acceptance of Protestant ideas, Knox moved to become tutor to the sons of two other Lothian lairds who were strong supporters of the Protestant movement: Hugh Douglas of Longniddry and John Cockburn of Ormiston. The lairds were especially helpful to the Protestant preachers, since they could provide security against arrest by Cardinal Beaton, now in the saddle and cracking his whip. In 1544 he executed five people for crimes which ranged from dishonouring the Virgin to breaking a fast by eating goose. The network of sympathetic lairds provided a system of safe houses akin to the Resistance in Occupied France during the Second World War. The strength of the Protestant movement varied from region to region. It was weak in the hinterland of Aberdeen in the north-east, due to the strong Catholic influence of the Earl of Huntly, but strong in Tayside, mid-way down the east coast. In the south-west in Dumfries and Galloway there was a Reform movement dating back to the days of the Lollards, itinerant preachers who taught Protestant principles, such as the supreme authority of Scripture, as early as the fourteenth century. The Highlands were never won over to the same extent and it was not until the conversion of the Earl of Argyll in the late 1540s that the cause made any impact in the far west. The Lothian lairds with whom Knox had become involved were inevitably of the Anglo-Protestant group. Some were 'assured

Scots' in the pay of Henry VIII, and others were persuaded by personal conviction. Theirs was a dangerous game and in the tense and unstable atmosphere of 1544 there were few citizens who did not carry some form of weapon, including priests, who were not supposed to carry arms of any kind.

When George Wishart, spearhead of the Protestant preachers, travelled around the country it was a cloak and dagger operation. In 1545 this charismatic orator returned to Dundee to preach during an attack of plague, choosing to stand on the city wall known as the Cowgate so that the plague victims could hear. Such public acts of defiance were bound to attract attention. Cardinal Beaton had a Fife priest, John Wigton, in his custody and bribed him with a pardon to stab Wishart after one of the services. Confronted by this wretched fellow, Wishart grabbed his wrist and disarmed him before setting him free. It was not long before the Cardinal made a further move against him, for when the preacher moved north to his home town of Montrose he found a fake letter from Lord Kinnear requesting a visit to his home in Angus, and learned that armed men were lying in wait for him *en route*. Wishart set out for his next destination in East Lothian. When he landed at Leith the nobles from the south-west who had invited him to meet them in Edinburgh did not show up. Instead he was offered protection by a posse of lairds from East Lothian who welcomed him ashore. Wishart chose to hand the sword to an intense young man who had recently joined the movement and was eager to play his part. John Knox was thirty and the month was December 1545.

2

The Double-Edged Sword

Before beginning the story of John Knox we must look at him in the context of his own times, if we are to make any sense of him. Europe in 1500 was on the brink of fundamental change. The static, medieval, feudal world in which pope, Holy Roman Emperor and king or queen reigned supreme was for the first time seriously called into question. Externally Christian Europe, or Christendom, was ranged around by the Islamic empire and looked towards a hostile frontier to the south and east. In the west the discovery of the New World, however, Spain had the exclusive permission of the pope to colonise and established immense possibilities for European trade and colonisation. This in turn increased the importance of Europe's merchant classes. The traditional rivals among the nation states, France and England, as yet had no colonies and looked to the new mercantile class to provide their rulers with loans to finance the power plays and wars through which they might extend their dominions.

The two other big players who dominated the game were the Pope and the Holy Roman Emperor. The Emperor previously ruled a major slice of central Europe, but when Charles I of Spain became the Emperor Charles V (1516-56), founding the Habsburg dynasty, he created an axis which stretched from Spain through the Netherlands to the German States. This posed a threat to the ambitions of France and resulted in a series of wars, with the papacy joining in to help drive the French out of north Italy. The French King, Francis I (1515-47), and his

son Henry II (1547-59) belonged to the increasingly powerful
House of Lorraine and Guise, which figures largely in the story
of John Knox.

War and trade were not the only means open to the kings
of Europe of expanding their power. Marriages between the
royal houses created new alliances and when in 1509 Henry VIII
of England (1509-47) married Catherine of Aragon, widow of
his brother Arthur, the union allied him with Spain, the Pope
and the Emperor against England's old enemy France. The
French had their own alliances of blood during this period.
Henry II married the Italian heiress Catherine of Medici, and
their daughter Elizabeth was the second wife of Philip II of
Spain, who was first married to Mary I of England, daughter
of Henry VIII. Their son Francis I of France (1559-60) married
Mary Queen of Scots, daughter of the marriage of James V of
Scotland (1513-42) to Mary of Guise. The family tree (p. 190)
together with the map (p. xi) shows that Scotland, despite its
position on the fringe of the rich and powerful kingdoms of
Europe and its relatively underdeveloped culture and economy,
had a part to play in the power game in Europe, usually on the
side of France. It suited the Scots to ally themselves with a
powerful enemy of England who would lend them support in
their continual wars and skirmishes with their larger neighbour;
and it equally suited the French, who were thereby granted
back-door access to England.

In all of this the Roman Catholic Church played a dominant
role. As well as head of the wealthiest organisation in Europe,
the Pope was temporal head of the Papal States in Italy. When
Clement VI issued the bull *Unam Sanctam* in 1302, he claimed
for the papacy supremacy over the kings of Christendom in the
temporal as well as the spiritual sphere. His successors had
difficulty in enforcing their claims over the competing kings
of Europe, but the church held huge estates throughout Europe
and commanded a bureaucracy in its clergy which vastly
outnumbered any of the armies or civil services of the countries
which made up Europe. The church was a multi-national
corporation less accountable to the nations in which it operated
than any modern international conglomerate. When it came to
collecting the land taxes and ecclesiastical dues, the papacy was

rich beyond the treasure of any king. For instance, in Scotland in the mid-sixteenth century the annual revenue of the church was nearly half that of the whole kingdom. The Crown took a mere £17,000 compared with £300,000 collected by the church.

Rulers dealt with this situation on the basis that if they could not beat them, they joined them. It was often the practice of kings to appoint their illegitimate offspring to wealthy benefices in order to keep their hands on the money (as long as they could get the dispensation for them to be ordained below the canonical age of twenty-four). For example Scotland's primate, Archbishop Alexander Stewart of St Andrews, was ordained at the age of eleven at the behest of his half-brother James IV and died alongside him in full armour when in 1513 the Scots were annihilated by an English army at Flodden. This widespread practice, along with simony (a person holding several benefices and taking the income while a lowly and often ill-qualified priest fulfilled the parish duties), resulted in widespread contempt and hostility towards the church in Scotland. Another abuse was the appointment of a lay commendator who was not ordained but received the income from a benefice. This proved a profitable means by which the nobility derived a share of the church's huge income.

The church had no problem recruiting for the priesthood. In fact there were too many priests. Various estimates of Scotland's population in the sixteenth century put it between 500,000 and 800,000 but even accepting the higher figure there were more than 3,000 priests – the equivalent of 20,000 out of 5 million in modern Scotland. Those who pursued a career in the medieval church had few sacrifices to make and their position in society guaranteed them many privileges, including inducements of the flesh. In such a church, where bishops flaunted their mistresses and only a minority were dedicated to a truly spiritual life, vows of poverty and celibacy were nothing but a bad joke.

Contempt for the church had become a rising tide in Europe by the beginning of the sixteenth century but it burst through the dykes at different times in different places, ebbing and flowing as events unfolded. Germany became Lutheran ten years before England broke with Rome. The passing of the next ten years saw a backlash in Germany against the Anabaptists, who based their teaching on Scripture but whose leadership claimed the influence of the Holy Spirit and was thought to be anarchic. Elsewhere in Europe the counter-Reformation (marked by the formation of the Jesuit Order in 1534) was well under way. Thus by the time that the Reformation reached Scotland in 1560 the floodtide unleashed by Luther in 1517 had been considerably muddied. It was still not clear whether the changes brought about by the Reformation were irreversible or whether the tide might turn back in favour of Rome.

Two factors distinguished the world after 1500 from the preceding age. First a new humanist emphasis in philosophy provided an intellectual basis for reform. The emerging middle class was able to use these ideas to question the right of the institutions of church and state to behave as they did. Even a somewhat backward country in northern Europe, such as Scotland, had its share of scholars who had studied at Europe's leading universities. Foremost among them in the early sixteenth century was John Major, who taught at Paris from 1526 to 1531 and on his return to Scotland in 1531 is likely to have influenced Knox. One of Major's works deals with legitimate rights of citizens against rulers, but his ideas on this were in line with moderate humanists like Erasmus, who had little appetite for revolution or reformation. Major's style belonged to the old world of the medieval schoolmen who argued in propositions which were 'proved' in logical manner. Knox shows a debt to this method at times but his distinctive contribution was to push the right to resist an ungodly ruler further than Major ever envisaged. Knox broke the mould of the scholastics and humanists who had come before him, who would probably have been appalled by how far he was prepared to put theory into practice.

The second crucial factor which helped spread protestantism was the invention and widespread use of the printing press. Without it Luther could have not achieved his Reformation. One has only to consider that a man preaching his way round Germany on horseback would have reached only a fraction of those who in reality read his printed sermons and pamphlets. Bibles were printed, first in Greek and then, as translations became available in national languages, for popular consumption. Protestant literature was regarded as subversive. While Knox was at university in the 1530s it was illegal to teach the Scriptures in Greek in Scotland. The English Reformer William Tyndale was forced into exile in 1524 and executed in 1536, as a result of his masterly English translation of the Bible (which eventually formed the backbone of the Authorised Version published in 1611).

In Scotland the traffic in ideas and people was most closely associated with the east coast. Trade with Germany, Antwerp and the Bordeaux ports of France (Calais, Rouen and Dieppe) made it easy for this underground literature to enter the stretch of coast from Aberdeen to Edinburgh, which included the ecclesiastical and intellectual centre of St Andrews. The area known today as Tayside was always strong in support of the Protestant cause, particularly among the lairds (Scottish landowners of the upper-middle class). William Lord Ruthven, Provost of Perth (the Scots equivalent of Lord Mayor), and John Erskine, Laird of Dun, were respected supporters of Lutheran ideas in the thirties and forties, together with Fife lairds such as Sir James Kirkcaldy of Grange, Sir James Learmonth of Dairsie, Provost of St Andrews, and the brilliant lawyer Henry Balnaves of Halhill. Evidence of wide support for this popular Protestant uprising surfaced in incidents such as the refusal of a majority of burgesses of Perth to pay their dues to the local clergy in 1527 and 1528.

The Reformers from this area were not lacking in a sense of humour. The Wedderburn brothers of Tayside (who later found it expedient to emigrate) produced the *Good and Godly Ballads*, which combined sacred songs with savage satire of the Roman Church. Its approach was echoed in 1540 in the satirical play *The Three Estates*, performed before James V and written by Sir David Lindsay, himself to play an influential role behind the scenes of the Scottish Reformation.

Protestantism gained its first martyr in 1528 when Archbishop James Beaton tricked a monk named Patrick Hamilton (who had become a Lutheran during his education at Wittenburg) into coming to St Andrews for a disputation. It ended with his being tried and burnt as a heretic within twelve hours of his arrest. The manner of his execution appalled the onlookers. In the cold, wet February weather gunpowder was added to the funeral pyre to fan the flames, but it blew away half his face. His heroic demeanour in meeting his end left a lasting impression on the onlookers. Knox later reports that one of the Archbishop's advisers warned him, 'If you will burn them, let them be burned in deep cellars; for the reek [smell of the smoke] of Master Patrick Hamilton has infected as many as it blew upon.'

Not all Scottish protestantism came out of idealism and conviction. The Lothian lairds, whose estates lay on the path of marauding English armies, which Henry VIII had a habit of sending into Scotland, were more ambivalent. Some received English money as paid retainers of the English monarch (who in 1527 had broken with Rome and in 1534 put himself at the head of a Protestant Church of England). Thus in some areas of Scotland to be pro-Protestant was to be pro-English and therefore unpatriotic, since Scotland's independence was perceived to be guaranteed by the Auld Alliance with France. Many of the nobility took the English shilling for less than noble ideals and the rest were content to receive their cut of church patrimony, seeing no need for reform of the system. In the first half of the sixteenth century Scotland was an unhappy, uncivilised and uncertain nation.

In a society where so much store was laid by kingship it had proved disastrous that in the fifteenth and sixteenth centuries in Scotland there were seven occasions when a child succeeded to the throne. The resulting struggle for advancement among the leading nobles created uncertainty and discontinuity. In Scotland the earls of Arran, Huntly and Argyll (respectively heads of the families of Hamilton, Gordon and Campbell) had their family domains respectively in the south-west, north-east and west of the country, while the tempestuous earls of Angus (Douglas) and Bothwell (Hepburn) held theirs in the east. The Hamiltons and their rivals the Lennox Stewarts were closest in blood-line to the throne. The Royal Stewart house had held the throne for two centuries but their hold on the crown was looking increasingly precarious without a well-founded succession.

The years which followed the death of James IV and the flower of Scottish nobility at Flodden on September 9 1513 gave ample opportunity for the noble families to exploit the power vacuum created by a boy king. As James V grew to maturity he inherited a kingdom bankrupted by his mother, Margaret Tudor, James IV's widow, who had married the Earl of Angus after Flodden. He cast around for a lucrative marriage, resisting his uncle Henry VIII's offer of a union with his daughter Mary Tudor. Henry and the Pope formed an unholy alliance against his next choice, the Pope's niece Catherine de Medici – the Pope because such an alliance was too far from home to be of use to him, and Henry because it was too near home and close to Rome. So James opted for the old policy of alliance with France, and married Madeleine, daughter of Francis I, but her health was so frail that she lasted less than a year in the bleak Scottish climate. He went again to France in 1538 and contracted a second marriage, to Mary of Guise, recently widowed at the age of twenty-two, who left her rich and powerful family, and her infant son, to come to Scotland. She brought with her the negotiator of the marriage, David Beaton, simultaneously Abbot of Arbroath and Bishop of Mirepoix in Languedoc. Beaton's education in France had fitted him well for the role of heir apparent to the primacy of Scotland. The influence of Francis I (who was brother both of Mary and of Charles, Cardinal of Lorraine) duly ensured that he got the job, along with Scotland's first cardinal's hat.

An heir for the throne was expected from Mary of Guise. James V actively consorted with other women, but he also paid court to his wife and in May 1540 Prince James was born, followed by Prince Robert in April 1541. Within days of the second birth both babies died, plunging James into a deep depression. He was closely reliant on Cardinal Beaton, who had become as useful to him as Cardinal Wolsey was to Henry VIII prior to the break with Rome. We can speculate whether James was ever tempted to emulate Henry and create a separate Scottish Church with himself at its head. The opportunity never arose. James was back at the point his father had reached before Flodden, his kingdom closely bound to France and on a collision course with England. The clash came when Henry VIII travelled north to meet him at York in September 1541. Fearing he would be won over to a pro-English, anti-papal policy, Cardinal Beaton and the Scottish bishops persuaded him not to go, first offering the excuse of bereavement over his sons' deaths, then in the summer of 1542, when the Queen again became pregnant, her confinement. The tyrannical Henry saw this as an opportunity to teach the Scots that he was not to be snubbed in this way, and declared war. It is a measure of Beaton's place in the realm that he was put in charge of one of the two armies. He proceeded to prosecute the battle as if it was a holy war against a country under papal interdict. Beaton's crusade ended in ignominy for the Scots at the battle of Solway Moss on November 25 1542, when 1,200 Scots were captured. The nobles among them were taken south to be browbeaten by Henry, whose policy towards his northern neighbour was consistently that of a savage bully.

James V's melancholia became suicidal and, muttering prophesies of his own doom, he declared he would not see Christmas. He did not. At the age of thirty he turned his face to the wall and died on December 14 in the French-style palace he had built for himself at Falkland, Fife. Even when news was brought to him of the birth of a baby daughter, the future Mary Queen of Scots, it elicited the gloomy retort, 'Adieu, farewell, it came with a lass and it will pass with a lass'. This was an allusion to the origin of the Stewart dynasty when the daughter of Robert I (the Bruce) married Walter Stewart. The lass, who remained in Linlithgow Palace with her mother, was not expected to live.

The future of Scotland was now exceedingly precarious. Would England move in for the kill? Would the French defend their interest there? Would there be a battle for the succession among the Scottish nobles? The answer to the first question was that the English commander awaited orders from Henry before pressing home his advantage. Cardinal Beaton saw his chance to seize power and with the aid of a forged will declared that James V had appointed him Regent for the six-day-old Mary Queen of Scots. He was opposed successfully and then imprisoned by James Hamilton, Earl of Arran, who made himself Regent and concluded a treaty with England on July 1 1543. The most important clause provided for Henry's young son Prince Edward to marry the infant Queen of Scots. The Scots were reluctant to agree to a further provision that the Queen should be taken to England. They had every reason to be distrustful of Henry's motives, since the independence of a queen could easily be eclipsed and subsumed in marriage, as could her kingdom.

The question of relations between church and state in Scotland came up in a curious way at this time. Henry balked at the suggestion of one of his commanders that English Bibles should be sent to the Scots Protestants, since he had just banned reading the Bible in English on pain of death (May 1543). Henry had the intention of regulating religion by means of a new formulary to be known as the King's Book, which he promised Arran he would send to Scotland. His reasoning was that it would then no longer be necessary for Scots to bother with the Bible [JR33].

This foreshadows the conflict between Bible and Prayer Book, the source of so much mutual misunderstanding and hostility between Scots and English religion in the future. In England the settlement between church and state after the Reformation treated canon law as a sub-section of the laws of the realm. Religion was regulated religion like any other area of activity. In Scotland the powers of the church were seen as deriving from the rights of godly people. This made the church an alternative source of authority alongside the state, a counter-balance, rather than subject to it. Ultimately this radical difference explains why Knox's ideas were better suited to Scotland than England. It also explains why the English Puritans (who shared Knox's views) could not dig the Anglican system out of the foundations of the English state and eventually emigrated rather than submit.

One direct consequence of the new treaty with England was that the Scottish Protestants changed overnight from a persecuted sect to protégés of the government. They were even encouraged by the Regent to rise against the Roman Catholic Church and in Dundee that summer of 1543 a mob looted the friaries. But when Arran tried to subvert Edinburgh to the Protestant cause he found it a more difficult proposition. The citizens rejected him as a heretic who had sold out to Henry, and his hold on events began to slip badly. The treaty was ratified at Holyrood Palace on August 25. But at this point Mary of Guise and Cardinal Beaton were handed a perfect ally in the person of Arran's half-brother, James Hamilton, Abbot of Paisley. Newly returned from France, Hamilton convinced Arran of the serious consequences of rending the Auld Alliance with France which had served them so well. Around the same time Matthew Stewart, Earl of Lennox (and next in line after the Regent for the throne), was preparing to come back from France and make his own bid for the throne. Panicked by this threat from the Catholic party, Arran began to see his dreams of a dynasty being thwarted by Lennox and the French. In his desperation he hit on a plan. If the infant Queen did not marry the heir to the English throne, why should she not marry a Hamilton and keep the succession in his family? That temptation persuaded the unstable Arran to execute a volte-face. He struck a deal with Beaton on September 3, repudiated the marriage contract and expelled the English ambassador, Sir Ralph Sadler. Then he set off for Stirling with Beaton to join the Queen and her mother, Mary of Guise, who by now had formed the opinion that Arran was 'the most inconstant person' she had known. Arran sought absolution for his heresies at the Franciscan convent in Stirling, and the baby Mary was crowned Queen at Stirling on September 9 1543.

Henry's response was as swift as it was terrible. The English army rased Edinburgh to the ground in the spring of 1544 and went home via Berwick, laying waste the countryside as it went. Then they waited for the Scottish harvest to be gathered by the tenant farmers, whose rent was paid in crops to the nobility and lairds, before striking again. It is estimated that English armies crossed the border two or three times a week between November 1544 and September 1545 to burn and pillage Scottish towns and villages. Henry's 'assured Scots', the ones in his pay, who had undertaken to punish their tenants on his orders, were far from popular.

Protestantism once more went into eclipse, but the brief spring it had enjoyed under Arran had yielded one important development. Along with the nobles released from custody in England, who now came back to Scotland, were exiled Protestant preachers who were anxious to sow the seeds of Lutheranism and the new version of protestantism developed in Switzerland. The town of Haddington in East Lothian had been burnt by the English army on May 17 1544, and many charred buildings stood as a reminder of Henry's wrath. It was here at this time that an idea was planted in the mind of the young priest and apostolic notary John Knox, which was to change the face of Scotland in future years.

Writing about these events twenty years later, Knox interpreted them from the English point of view. Despite the fact that many of them were likely to have been burnt as heretics in Henry's England, the Scots Protestants at this time regarded England as their protector and Cardinal Beaton as the arch-traitor. Beaton became the focus of their resentment for his oppressive tactics. In Perth a mob of citizens tried to copy the Dundee protest of the year before, but were ruthlessly dealt with, one woman's suckling infant being plucked from her before she was executed by drowning.

As we have seen, not all the Protestant supporters could be described as having the highest motives. Lennox had joined them. Seeking a base for his claim to the throne and following his family's policy of always taking the opposite side to the Hamiltons, Lennox made his own alliance with England by marrying Henry VIII's niece Margaret Douglas. (Their son Henry, Lord Darnley, was destined to make his own mark on Anglo-Franco-Scottish affairs.) The Protestant group was now an incongruous mixture of duplicitous and power-mad nobles, idealistic lairds like Balnaves and Erskine of Dun, and a motley collection of clerics and discontents. One of the common topics of discussion by the more desperate among them was a plot to assassinate Cardinal Beaton. How far this was generally known among the preachers who travelled Scotland spreading Protestant ideas from the pulpit can only be guessed. But it can be said with certainty that becoming a Protestant in those dangerous times was not the soft option. Against this background Knox makes his entrance carrying a two-handed sword, as the bodyguard of the fiery preacher George Wishart.

3

Martyrdom and Murder

When Wishart stepped ashore at Leith in early December 1545, he entered a murder conspiracy: not only the threat of his own murder by Cardinal Beaton but also a long-rehearsed plan to kill Beaton himself. Whether Wishart was part of the plot has never been conclusively proved, but on April 17 1544 agents of Henry VIII wrote from Newcastle to say that a Scot named 'Wyssehart' had come to them with letters from John Crichton, the Laird of Brunston, intimating that the Protestant lairds of Fife were willing to ambush the Cardinal and kill him when he was passing through their area. They wanted money to raise a small army to sack church properties, and to be granted asylum in England, which was then a haven for Protestants fleeing persecution. Henry promised £1,000 in return for the assassination, which would have removed one of his most able opponents north of the border. One of Crichton's letters had been written from Cockburn's house in Ormiston and both these men were among the group who met Wishart at Leith [Percy, p. 36; Reid, p. 27].

The spotlight has not stayed on George Wishart's possible involvement in the assassination of Cardinal Beaton, for two reasons. The first is that Wishart's execution has usually been taken as a catalyst for the murder of the Cardinal, and so the longstanding plot has been overlooked. The second reason is that Wishart has been portrayed as too spiritual to be involved in murderous work. He is cast as the pious preacher, the saintly chorus who left the stage before the main drama.

Wishart hailed from the north-east of Scotland and graduated *magna cum laude* from the University of Louvain in 1532 (not exactly a hot-bed of Protestant ideas: four years earlier the university authorities had written to congratulate St Andrews on the burning of Patrick Hamilton). He taught Greek in Erskine of Dun's school in Montrose, where he broke the law by using Erasmus's New Testament. Before action could be taken against him he went to England, and again got into trouble preaching Lutheran ideas in Bristol and was forced to recant. He then spent time in Germany and Switzerland, where he translated the new Swiss Confession into English. Returning to Corpus Christi College in Cambridge, he was described there by a contemporary as 'courteous, lowly, lovely, glad to teach and desirous to learn' and by Knox as 'a man of such graces as before him were never heard in this realm'. That does not sound like the portrait of an assassin.

But if there was something charismatic about Wishart there was also something of the quiet fanatic, the gleaming-eyed zealot who would not shrink from violence as a means of purification of society. He was known to purify himself by washing in a bath-tub every night, which must be reckoned zealous by the standards of the sixteenth century. He was given to violent sessions of personal prayer on his knees, when he would weep and rock forward, burying his face, as happened one night at the house of James Watson in Invergowrie [Knox, I, 60-5].

The tall, gaunt Wishart with the close-cropped hair and long black beard was a fiery soul who burned with a cause. When two friars once disrupted his sermon, he lashed out at them as 'sergeants of Satan'. Should it be all that surprising if he regarded the removal of Cardinal Beaton, the personification of all he despised in the medieval church, as nothing more than an act of righteousness? Percy writes eloquently: 'There was about (Beaton) the flavour of the Italian Renaissance tyrant; statesman and inquisitor; sumptuous and ruthless, with his guards and his ladies and his seven bastard children.' On a very human level, Wishart knew that Beaton was determined to kill him, and it would not have been strange for him to have entertained the thought of arranging Beaton's death. It is evident that Wishart was wooed and respected by the Lothian lairds,

rough diamonds as some of them may have been. Would they
not have confided their plot to him? It is asking us to believe
that he was a holy innocent, a naïve tool in their hands, if he
did not know of and approve their plan.

Whether or not he knew of the Crichton plot, Wishart was
anguished as he neared the climax of his preaching tour of
Lothian at Haddington on January 12 1546. On this bitterly cold
Tuesday, the attendance at the first service had been surprisingly
small and Wishart was uneasy. His suspicions were confirmed
when a boy arrived with a letter from some prominent Protestants
in the west of Scotland which said they could not now make their
rendezvous with him in Edinburgh. The preacher sensed that
Cardinal Beaton was about to make his move.

Patrick Hepburn, Earl of Bothwell (father of the third
husband of Mary Queen of Scots) was the chief noble in the
Lothians, Beaton's ally, and as Knox puts it, 'made for money
butcher to the Cardinal'. The word was out that Bothwell was
about to arrest Wishart. Hence the low church attendance.
Wishart sensed that he did not have much time. After reading
the letter and pacing the church for half an hour, he turned
to Knox and confessed that 'he wearied of the world, for he
perceived that men began to weary of God'. He took his leave
of his hosts and when Knox volunteered to travel with the party
to Ormiston House, Wishart uttered the memorable line, 'Nay,
return to your bairns. One is sufficient for a sacrifice.' Knox
reluctantly handed back the two-handed sword with which he
had been furnished in his role of bodyguard.

At midnight Bothwell surrounded the house with 500 men,
and after making a promise not to hand Wishart over to the
Cardinal took him to his castle at Elphinstone, where Beaton
was waiting. (In his history Knox makes light of the treachery
of Bothwell; but at the time he wrote the younger Bothwell was
riding high and the old feudal tie of his family to the Bothwells
perhaps stayed his hand.) The Cardinal ordered the lairds also
to be seized, but on hearing the soldiers approaching Ormiston
House Crichton fled through the woods to the Douglas
stronghold of Tantallon Castle where he took refuge.

Cockburn of Ormiston and John Sandilands of Calder were
arrested and taken to Edinburgh Castle. Cockburn escaped in

broad daylight by climbing over the wall and down the castle rock. Sandilands slipped his bonds just as effectively by bribing Beaton. Wishart was not so lucky. He was imprisoned in the 'bottle' dungeon of St Andrews Castle, now strongly fortified to keep the Cardinal's plundered treasure and to ensure that he would never again be caught out as he was three years previously when Arran made his bid for the Regency. Beaton held three strong cards: the Lord Governor Arran's eldest son was in his safe-keeping at St Andrews; the Queen Mother, Mary of Guise, was his firm ally together with her powerful friends in France; and Wishart, the leading Protestant preacher, was in his power.

St Andrews Castle sits low on a rocky finger of land, on the hill where a church was first established by Celtic monks 1,000 years previously. Dominating the site was one of Europe's most impressive cathedrals, begun in 1178 and completed in 1316, and winding down from it a cliff road led to the pier and the harbour. Between the castle and the cathedral, Wishart was tied to a stake, strangled and burnt on March 1 1546. The letters GW are set in the road on the spot where he died, a short walk from the cobbles outside St Salvator's clock-tower, where the letters PH mark the funeral pyre of Patrick Hamilton.

Although the Protestants were still a minority and a mixed bunch of idealists, opportunists and thugs, the death of Wishart gave them a martyr. The tide of dissent against Beaton was rising. The man who preached the sermon at Wishart's trial, John Winram, Sub-Prior of St Andrews, was destined to become a Protestant (and one of the new kirk's first superintendents). Wishart was impressed enough to ask Winram to pay a pastoral visit before his execution. The prior for whom he was acting was the fifteen-year-old illegitimate son of James V, Lord James Stewart, a 'lay' prior, also destined to become a leading supporter of the cause, and an eventual Regent of Scotland as Earl of Moray.

It now became inevitable that the plan to assassinate Beaton would be put into action. It took less than two months. On May 29 1546 a party of sixteen men waited until the Cardinal's mistress, Marion Ogilvy, had departed by the postern gate in the early hours of the morning. Just as the first shift of masons and builders were beginning work on the castle fortifications, William Kirkcaldy, the Laird of Grange, approached a sentry and asked if the Cardinal was yet awake. The man became suspicious and was stabbed and tossed into the moat. The conspirators, led by Norman and John Leslie, sons of the Earl of Rothes, hustled into the castle and showed out the workmen. By this time an alarm had been raised. Beaton and his page boy barricaded themselves in his bedroom with furniture, only to see smoke billowing under the door as the intruders applied a brazier of coals to it. Beaton opened the door, pleading that they could not kill him since he was a priest. John Leslie and Peter Carmichael of Balmadie ignored his pleas and stabbed him with their 'whingers' (small daggers). The third assassin, James Melville, sought to turn the act into an execution for the murder of his friend Wishart by calling on Beaton to repent before running him through twice. Beaton allegedly cried, 'I am a priest, fye, fye!' before moaning, 'All is gone', and expiring. What followed is brutal. They hung the body outside the castle window for all to see, and the historian Pitscottie records that 'ane called Guthrie pished in his mooth'. The body was then salted and thrown into the bottle dungeon, which had not long since housed Wishart.

It was more than murder. It was a *coup d'état*, the first step of a revolution, and it is significant that the Leslies and their fellow-conspirators were charged with high treason. Even more astonishing was the fact that Beaton's killing did not bring immediate retribution. The Scottish government, led by Arran, was frozen in inactivity. It held back for two principal reasons. Firstly, Arran knew that those holding St Andrews Castle, the 'Castilians' as they were later styled, were holding his eldest son as hostage. Secondly, the option of summoning the French fleet was not open, since six days after Beaton's death the French had agreed to English peace terms at Camp de Calais. Although no Scots had been represented at the discussions, Francis I of France had chosen to make a separate peace, which would include Scotland only if it agreed to honour the broken marriage treaty of 1543, which provided for the Queen of Scots to marry the heir to the English throne. Wary of English troops crossing the border, Arran began to assemble an army all through the summer of 1546, while the Castilians played merry hell in St Andrews.

Within days Kirkcaldy of Grange and James Melville had brought in men to swell the garrison to well over 100. Originally it had been mainly Fife lairds who were involved in the coup. Strangely the Tayside Protestants seem to have kept themselves at arm's length, leading one historian to conclude that the principal motive of some of the Fife lairds may have been to acquire Beaton's gold rather than to advance the Protestant cause. The Lothian lairds, who might have been expected to be in the forefront of the action, also showed reluctance to become involved. Cockburn and Crichton, with Sandilands, had other things on their minds, since they had been summoned for trial on charges of assisting Wishart.

Although the news of Beaton's death caused a certain amount of glee throughout Europe (particularly for Henry VIII and the Emperor Charles V, both of whom delighted in the setback to French dominion in Scotland), it also had the effect of uniting what was left of leadership among the nobility of Scotland. No longer able to count on French intervention, Mary of Guise, Arran and the nobles closed ranks around the infant Queen in a way that would have been difficult to imagine a year previously. They agreed that the little Queen would marry neither Henry VIII's son Prince Edward nor Arran's son. Formal proceedings for treason were begun against thirty-four named conspirators and their goods and lands were ordered forfeit by August. At the same time Arran decreed that four areas of Scotland would take turns to provide troops to besiege the castle. Quarrels had arisen about who would pay the bill. Since the situation had arisen from the murder of a prelate, the church was asked to pay £3,000 a month to finance the siege. At the end of August engineers began to tunnel towards the castle and the Castilians responded by digging a counter-mine to intercept their tunnel and block it. (Both can be examined when touring the castle, and the entrance to the first tunnel still exists beneath a manhole a few yards from the GW motif in the road.)

Arran and his troops made heavy weather of the siege. There was no sign of an English or French intervention and Knox began seriously to think of leaving Scotland. A new archbishop had been appointed, in the person of Arran's illegitimate brother, John Hamilton. He was not as despotic as Beaton but was pro-French and it would be only a matter of time before he moved against Wishart's supporters. Lutheran Germany crossed Knox's mind as a possible refuge but he resisted the idea of England, he says, because popish practices remained in force under Henry VIII despite the break with Rome.

If the circumstantial evidence points to Wishart as part of the assassination plan, was Knox guilty by association and also privy to the plot? It has never been in question that he approved of it. Even allowing for the fact that when he wrote his history of these events in 1566 he felt bitter and alienated, he had also reached a point in his own thinking when he believed that the removal of a tyrant was a 'godly act'. There is no suggestion that he was shocked that his comrades could have done such a thing. He wrote in a harsh and cynical way about Beaton's assassination, even pausing to make crude jokes about the Archbishop of Glasgow whom Beaton had invited to witness Wishart's execution from a velvet-draped dais.

Knox makes no mention of having any foreknowledge of the plot, but it should be remembered that in 1545 he was a junior recruit to the Protestant ranks as tutor to their 'bairns', and would not necessarily have been taken into the confidence of the plotters. Knox was not yet a leader. He had not yet been blooded as a preacher for the cause and one interpretation of Wishart's farewell words to him could well have been 'Save yourself while you can, friend. You haven't done anything to die for.'

The death of Wishart had stunned Knox. He felt the guilt that all disciples feel when their leader has been executed and they remain alive. It was with terrible irony that he found himself studying with his pupils the passage in John's gospel in which Jesus is arrested in the Garden of Gethsemane and tells his disciple Peter to put up his sword, which is followed by Peter's denial of Jesus as he strives to save his own skin (John 18:1-27). The parallels between the gospel story and the situation in which he found himself with Wishart could not have escaped him. Wishart was the figure who did not pass the cup of woe which was offered to him. Knox was the disciple who put up his sword and was now thinking of fleeing to Germany to save his skin. Knox was confronted with a decision. Would it be cowardice to leave Scotland at this time and a betrayal of the principles that Wishart had died for?

He does not write anywhere of a moment of conversion. Not all conversions are the blinding light which St Paul experienced. In any case the religious tradition which stresses personal conversion and the importance of making an emotional commitment to Christ would have been alien to Knox. He thought that there were absolute truths, to which the Bible was the supreme testimony, and that godliness was a question of perceiving these and applying them to life. Personal feelings did not enter into the question of discovering truth. Thus he would not have been likely to make much of his inner emotions. But there are a number of pointers that Knox made a fundamental commitment at this time and that it was precipitated by the parallel between the story of the Garden of Gethsemane and the arrest of Wishart. Years later when he was on his death-bed he asked his wife to read to him from this very passage of Scripture (John 18), adding that it was 'where I first cast my anchor'. He recognised that his spiritual voyage had first begun with this passage. It affords the key to the inner heart of Knox's religion and the point at which he realised that he could not desert the cause that he had joined. But should he take the further step and join the rebels in the castle of St Andrews? Before he could bring himself to answer that question, it was decided for him.

4

The Castilians

Knox admits that the next stage of the journey, a short sail across the Forth and round to St Andrews, was not even his idea. The fathers of his pupils suggested that their tutor might be safer among his Protestant friends in the castle and that their sons would benefit from the experience. The Castilians had managed to obtain supplies locally from a friendly laird and in November another supply ship arrived from England. It returned to London with Norman Leslie and Henry Balnaves on board. Although the latter had been one of the judges in the Court of Session who passed sentence on the Castilians in August, his sympathies lay with the Protestants. When he defected to St Andrews Castle, he was an important recruit, not least because of his skill as a negotiator. The two emissaries extracted substantial promises of aid from Henry VIII to promote the Protestant cause in Scotland, and in return promised to deliver to him Arran's son and the infant Queen.

Meanwhile Arran was desperate to stave off an English invasion. Pressed by Mary of Guise, he negotiated a truce, which involved among other things sending to Rome for papal absolution for Beaton's murder, and the restoration of Norman Leslie as hereditary Sheriff of Fife. It was a bizarre farrago of double-dealing, neither side intending to keep its promises. No sooner had the Castilians bought more time with their truce than they sent an emissary to Henry VIII to block the papal absolution, itself a monumental piece of hypocrisy, since they had declared themselves utterly opposed to the tyranny of the Catholic Church.

For Arran's part, the Scottish Privy Council was preparing to ratify a request from Hamilton to bring to book all those who promoted Protestant heresies, which it duly did on March 19 1547.

Perhaps it was this last development that prompted Hugh Douglas of Longniddry to propose to Knox that he should think of heading for St Andrews, where the Castilians seemed to lead charmed lives. Neither man was aware that some of the rougher element among the Castilians were using the truce to foray into the town for orgies, in which they 'used their bodies in lechery with fair women, serving their appetite as they felt good' [Pitscottie, II, 86-7]. St Andrews, the ancient ecclesiastical capital of Scotland, was far from being the City of God. Here, facing one another across the clifftop road on which Wishart was martyred, were the rebels and the cathedral authorities. Life in St Andrews during Lent in 1547 must have been a bizarre and tense experience.

Most of the sites at which these events took place can still be seen today. The cathedral and the castle are ruins; but the visitor can walk from Beaton's castle to his cathedral along the cliff, which has been eroded by the march of tides. Climbing the stairs of St Rule's tower in the cathedral precinct gives an excellent view of the scene. To the east, directly ahead in the centre of the town, is the parish church, Holy Trinity, where, during the truce, clerics from both sides were preaching, often against each other. Behind the tower to the west is the sea, over whose horizon could come a French fleet to bring nemesis or an English one to bring succour. To the right, to the north, is the castle where the rebels were reaping the benefit of Beaton's mighty fortifications. And down below, to the left, enclosed by Prior Hepburn's great wall, completed not long after its foundation in 1512, is the site of St Leonard's College, now a school; in 1547 it stood beside the priory in the cathedral chapter. Here in this holy hectare Catholics and Protestants came face to face, ready to do military or ecclesiastical battle.

The verbal battle had already started in the form of public disputations, such as the one featured in Umberto Eco's book *The Name of the Rose*. It is hard for us to imagine a situation in which a debate about theological propositions could end with a man being tied to a stake, strangled and burnt. But it was axiomatic in the medieval world that the church was the divinely-appointed vehicle for saving people from the hell that lay beneath life and fitting them for the heaven that lay beyond it. There was no salvation outside the church. If heretics were allowed to set up a system which challenged that authority, the whole edifice would be undermined. St Thomas Aquinas compared the heretic to a counterfeiter and argued that he should be put to death. What was at stake was absolute truth, something that only vociferous minorities dare claim to possess today, but which, then, it was assumed could be discerned by reason, by propositions and by dialectical argument.

The sermons of the time (Knox's included) are often a mixture of abstract arguments which border on the turgid but which give way to lurid and specific accusations. The strong language Knox used was not unusual for his time. People expected their preachers to be outspoken. The Protestant approach to salvation was that believers were saved by faith. This was a Pauline doctrine which Luther had made one of the pillars of his system as 'justification by faith alone'. This led them to challenge the system of pardons, indulgences, fasts and pilgrimages, since, they argued, it was not possible to acquire heavenly grace by performing acts or good works. Had the Catholic Church been able to argue that these were symbolic gestures or mystical acts whose significance God alone decided (as many Catholics would do nowadays), they might have defused the criticism. But they stood and fought on the battleground of absolutes, linking the real church on earth with the real church in heaven in a very concrete way. They argued that Jesus had said to Peter that (a) he would be given the 'keys' of the kingdom; and (b) whatsoever he did on earth would be done in heaven (Matt. 16:19). Thus Peter's successor, the pope, could command church practices which would be valid in heaven. The Protestant answer was to go back to the Scriptures and demolish the foundation on which the church had been built. The commission to Peter was not intended to set up a system, the Protestants argued, and since the pope had supplanted the Bible with his system he was Antichrist.

The mass was another fundamental issue. The sacrifice of the mass was valid because it was performed by a priest whose ordination was validated by the 'true' church, said Rome. The Protestants argued that Rome was effectively saying that a priest who was a sinner could repeat the redeeming act performed by Jesus on the cross by saying words over a wafer. Protestants still believed in ordaining men to administer sacraments (reduced from seven to two – baptism and Holy Communion). However, ministers were never regarded as having the same status as priests in the Catholic system, a divergence which still creates a gulf to church unity today, despite enormous ecumenical rapprochement. To the Protestant the church was necessary, to the Catholic it was *essential*.

The Catholic position was that church tradition was equal to Scripture and that the church was the ultimate authority on all matters, whereas the Protestants argued that Scripture was exclusively the foundation stone upon which all other church practices and doctrines must be built. The Protestants of the sixteenth century tend to appear fundamentalist in their attitude to the Bible, but it was not so much that they took the Bible literally as that they used it in a typological way to apply its prophecies to the situation of their own times (for example the whore of Babylon in the Book of Revelation applied to the papacy).

These were the conflicting teams which faced each other in St Andrews when Knox arrived just after Easter, in mid-April 1547. Refereeing the conflict was Sub-Prior John Winram, sympathetic to reform and eventually to join the Protestants, but under increasing pressure from the new archbishop to crack down on heretics. The attack from the pulpit of the parish church was being led by the Principal of St Leonard's College, Dean John Annand. From the same pulpit the Protestant case was being put by John Rough, whom we last met as Arran's chaplain preaching to Knox in Lothian, in the days before Arran's 'apostasy'. He was now acting as chaplain to the Castilians and could not have found it a very rewarding task. Indeed as he left soon afterwards there is every reason to believe that he wanted to get out and go back to England.

He was also making heavy weather of his task. When Knox turned up in the parish church catechising his pupils, and lecturing to them in the castle chapel on John's gospel, Rough was not slow to appreciate the way he handled words. He asked if Knox would supply him with some arguments against Dean Annand and was obviously pleased with what he got, since when Balnaves returned from the London negotiations the two men approached Knox to become the next chaplain at the castle. Knox immediately refused on the grounds that he had not received a 'lawful vocation'. Rough soon provided him with one. Preaching the following Sunday in the parish church he chose as his subject the election of ministers and, turning to Knox at the end of the sermon, asked him to accept appointment as a minister. The congregation indicated its approval.

'Whereat the said John, abashed, burst forth in abundant tears and withdrew himself to his chamber.' These are Knox's own words and they are most revealing about his character. They show a vulnerable man. When he wrote about his 'call' he was undoubtedly trying to show that he was not a self-appointed revolutionary, but the servant under God of those who followed the cause. That belief remained with him throughout his career and is an important key to understanding his thinking. His words also show that his reluctance to accept the call was genuine enough. He had missed arrest and death by a few hours when he handed the sword back to Wishart. Now he was being asked to go into the front line of the battle, but this time without a sword.

To say that Knox did not want to die is not to accuse him of cowardice. He was too shrewd not to see how slender the chances were of the rebellion's successful outcome. His experience of Wishart's 'betrayal' had shown him how little reliance could be placed on the moral strength of the conspirators and he must already have recognised that there were few saints among the prospective martyrs in the castle. Yet his tears of frustration betray that he knew he was cornered. Wishart had not passed the cup that night in Haddington, but here now was his disciple being offered the chance to deny the cause, as Peter had done after Gethsemane. The man who was currently lecturing about that very incident in John's gospel had a troubled conscience.

It must have got to work on him. A few days later when Dean Annand was preaching in the parish church Knox interrupted his sermon. Annand had claimed that the authority of the church was final in its condemnation of Lutherans and heretics. Knox

burst out that he could prove that the Catholic Church had
degenerated further from the purity of the days of the apostles
than the Jews had from the laws of Moses when they condemned
Jesus. Annand declined to debate with this upstart, but those
present called on him to make good his words, and the following
Sunday he mounted the same pulpit steps to deliver his first
sermon in public, before a congregation which included Winram
and many of the friars, as well as John Major and his university
colleagues.

Characteristically he met the challenge head-on, choosing a text
from Daniel 7, which is summarised in the *History* [I, 83-6]. He
began by accusing the papacy of being Antichrist, citing the lives
of some of the popes. He attacked pilgrimages and pardons under
the banner of the doctrine of justification by faith, concluding
with a challenge to anyone to take him up on any point which
was not based upon the truth of Scripture. Reaction to the sermon
included the comment, 'Others sned [cut off] the branches of
the papistry but he strikes at the root, to destroy the whole.' The
response of the professorial pew is not recorded, but it is probable
that if Knox showed anything of the swashbuckling style which
was to be his hallmark in the future, John Major may have had
something of the same reaction as Queen Victoria's to the
evangelist Dwight Moody when she declared it was not the sort
of religious performance that she liked.

The outcome was a summons from Winram to Rough and
Knox to attend a meeting with himself and several friars in St
Leonard's Yard. There he presented them with a list of the
heretical doctrines they were preaching. This was the accepted
form of a trial for heresy. Nevertheless the meeting seems to have
been conducted in a spirit of mutual respect. Knox and Winram
discussed whether or not a bishop who did not preach had a right
to the title and whether the church tithes rightly belonged to those
who took them. Knox made a fool of a friar called Arbuckle who
had argued that the apostles did not receive the Holy Spirit until
after they had set up their ceremonies. (This would have meant
that ceremonies were invented by men and not God – thus
conceding the nub of Knox's objection to them.) But Winram
had the last laugh by inviting a rota of 'orthodox' preachers from
the university and priory to take up all the Sunday slots in the

parish church, and so prevented Knox and Rough access to the pulpit. Knox responded by preaching on weekdays, thereby gathering around him an increased congregation for the communion service in the castle chapel on Sundays.

Knox has been criticised for giving the sacrament to Beaton's murderers. This seems a strange accusation, for at the time the old canons were not in use and the new Protestant order of communion had not yet been adopted. Knox always seems to have regarded the sermon as more central than the sacrament and for him the most important factor would have been the prophetic truth of their cause, rather than whether the liturgy was correct or his listeners were entitled to receive the sacrament. He did believe that Beaton's murder was justified, although he certainly took the chance to reprove many of the Castilians for their reprobate lives. Although Knox had now taken over from Rough, it is unlikely that he lived in the castle. During the truce he would have been more likely to have stayed with his pupils in a 'safe' house in the town. The month was now June and events beyond St Andrews meant that both sides were nearer a denouement.

On January 27 1547 Henry VIII died. Although Somerset, the Lord Protector to the young King Edward, had agreed to honour the agreement to send money and men to the Castilians, he had problems of his own in establishing a government and was forced to trim back his level of support. Then on March 27 the French king, Francis II, also died. He was succeeded by Henry II, a more militant Catholic, who not only cracked down on the French Protestants immediately, but saw a chance to use Scotland as the means to conquer England while it was weakened during the minority of Edward VI. Henry II's ambassador to Scotland, Sieur d'Oysel, brought Mary of Guise a promise to send help and to give the young Queen Mary a safe refuge in France. At this time the counter-Reformation was gathering force across Europe and protestantism was suffering setbacks. In January the Council of Trent had issued a ruling on justification which made a Protestant schism inevitable, and the Emperor Charles V had routed the German Protestants at the battle of Muhlberg. Against this background St Andrews Castle was looking less a beacon of hope and more a glowing ember that was about to be stamped out.

5

The Galley Slave

In April the papal absolution arrived in Scotland and was delivered to Arran. He delayed handing it over for a month, confident that, whether or not they accepted it, victory would soon be within his grasp. When the Castilians examined the absolution they noticed it contained the words *remittimus irremissibile* [we remit the irremissible] and used this as an excuse to reject it. They were buying time. Arran was happy to let them keep the absolution, since if they accepted its terms he would have them in his hands, and even if they did not, the arrival of French help would resolve the situation in his favour. For that matter, both sides were confident that their foreign allies would come to their aid. However the English were exasperated that the Castilians still had not sent their hostage, Arran's son, to England. Somerset decided it was better to make plans for a general invasion than to make the Castilians his priority. But before he could even begin to march northwards, twenty French galleons had left Rouen under the command of Leon Strozzi, who bore the title of Prior of Capua. Strozzi had left Italy with his brother Peter and both *émigrés* were now commanders, of the French navy and army respectively. Picking up fresh water at Tynemouth after forcing his way into harbour on July 5, Strozzi was in St Andrews by the time the French ambassador in London was informed that he had left Rouen. The irate English now began in earnest to collect an army at Newcastle. The truce was well and truly over.

The French fleet still kept the element of surprise – for even

Arran did not yet know they were there. They soon announced their presence. On arrival in the bay they bombarded the castle with their cannon but only succeeded in hitting a few houses nearby. The castle returned the fire and scored a hit on one of Strozzi's ships. Under cover of the fleet it limped round to the mouth of the river Tay and made repairs at Broughty Ferry, where a stout castle commanded the approach to Dundee on the north bank. Strozzi sent word to Arran who was mustering troops in the borders at Langholm, where he was preparing to repel the English invasion, now expected at the end of August. So Arran turned round and made for St Andrews with his army. The wilder Castilians were confident they could hold out until the English arrived, but Knox muttered grimly that their confidence was misplaced. He was right. On July 24 Arran arrived with his army in the town and Strozzi's fleet reappeared in the bay. The Castilians were caught between the devil and the deep blue sea.

Strozzi was not going to be caught twice in the same firing line, and was anxious to get the battle over before the English arrived. He had spotted that the Castilians were within range both of the abbey church and of St Salvator's, and remarked contemptuously that if they had had any military skill they would have left neither standing. Under cover of darkness, and using ropes and pulleys, he had cannon hauled on to the roofs of the abbey church and St Salvator's. At four in the morning on July 30 the cannon opened fire. After six hours, bombardment the south wall of the castle was breached. As if to say enough is enough, the skies yielded a torrential downpour which halted the bombardment. Strozzi was about to offer his galley slaves freedom if they volunteered as assault troops when William Kirkcaldy of Grange emerged from the castle to ask for surrender terms.

These were never written down but it is generally agreed that one of them was that the Castilians should not be handed over to Lord Arran. They stood a better chance with the French as prisoners than they would have on trial in Scotland for murder and treason. As for Knox, he would probably have been put on trial for heresy, since his three months as a preacher had given him a high profile and the content of his sermons would not have been forgotten or forgiven. It is not clear whether Knox was actually in the castle during the bombardment but, whether at his own request or that of Balnaves, he was taken by Strozzi into the galleys as one of 120 prisoners. Strozzi then proceeded to strip the castle of Cardinal Beaton's treasure, valued at £100,000, and to destroy most of the fortifications in case the English took it over.

The fleet then set sail for France. According to Knox's *History*, Strozzi had given a promise that when they reached France the prisoners would be set at liberty and free to go anywhere but Scotland. On the voyage they took care to avoid English ships, since France was not at war with England. At one point they ran aground on the Dogger Bank but eventually the French galleys sighted land at Fécamp near Dieppe, where the Scots could have expected to have found plenty of fellow-countrymen. However Strozzi took them on to Rouen, where the Scots gentry were dispersed to neighbouring towns, still under guard. Eventually, after persistently refusing to attend mass, most of them were sent to the fortress of Mont St Michel as conscientious objectors. As for Knox and the rest, they were bundled below decks to be chained to the oars as galley slaves.

Why did Strozzi not hand over his prisoners to Arran in St Andrews that day? It could not have been because he was hurrying to get away before the English arrived, since he spent a further week offshore destroying the castle. It would surely have been in accordance with his king's wishes, and those of Mary of Guise, to have made an example of the Cardinal-killers by executing them '*pour encourager les autres*'. Strozzi in fact struck a deal with Kirkcaldy which undoubtedly saved the lives of the Castilians, not one of whom was executed for his part in the murder or the siege. Perhaps it is simpler to believe that Strozzi was a professional military man with a streak of contempt for politicians and prelates. His concept of honour was to win the battle, take the prisoners and then treat them with dignity.

The inept Arran now had greater problems than the Castilians. In September an English fleet appeared in the Forth and an army of 12,000 men under Lord Protector Somerset and the Earl of Warwick crossed the border, demanding that the Scots comply with the marriage treaty of Greenwich. There was now no time for French help to be summoned, and in any event France was reluctant to precipitate a war with England. So Arran met the vanguard of the English army at Pinkie Cleugh, outside Musselburgh, while Protector Somerset waited near Knox's native East Lothian. The Scots assembled in a strong position on Edmonstone Edge, their pikemen bristling like a great hedgehog; but they needlessly threw away their tactical advantage by a premature forward charge. Thus, only five years after the rout of Solway Moss, the Scots were again massacred, losing as many as 7,000 men, while English casualties amounted to a few hundred. Somerset left Scotland on September 28 but kept a garrison fleet at Broughty Ferry, which successfully struck up an alliance with the Protestants of Tayside. Somerset reinstituted the 'assured Scots' policy in Lothian, where Knox's former patrons, Cockburn, Crichton and Douglas, were again happily taking the English shilling.

During the invasion the Queen and her mother were safe in Stirling Castle, except for one occasion: when the English forces threatened to move from Leith, between September 11 and 18, they went into hiding in the Augustinian priory on Inchmahome Island off the north shore of Lake Menteith.

Meanwhile Knox settled down to life as a galley slave. It was considered the next most severe punishment after execution to be given a life sentence in the galleys. Since Knox and the Castilians had not been sentenced by any court they did not know how long their torment would last. 'Torment' was the word Knox used to describe his situation, as well as 'affliction'. Yet he wrote surprisingly little about his time in the galleys. It must have put iron in his soul as well as his wrist; but as with bad experiences, the subconscious is all too ready to suppress the memory after they are over. Jasper Ridley gives interesting details about the general conditions in a French galley around this time [pp. 66-7]. The galley itself was between 100 ft and 150 ft long, 30 ft wide and stood only 6 ft above the water line, making it unsuitable for heavy seas, so that it could only sail the North Sea route to Scotland in summer. In winter the daily ration of soup, biscuit and water was supplemented by wine, and thus the two winters he spent on shore were probably the saving of Knox. The 150 galley slaves or 'forsairs' rowed six to the oar, and the twenty-five oars were about 45 ft long and passed through the sides of the ship. They were kept chained to the oar when not doing other duties such as sail-mending and were given a uniform consisting of a coarse brown tunic, a vest, two shirts and two pairs of canvas breeches. A red cap was issued, but shoes were only given out for shore duty, in case the *forsairs* tried to escape. Many were convicts, and others prisoners of war. A *'comite'* was there to make sure that they pulled their weight and in each section of the ship *sous-comites* who carried whips.

The *comites* on Knox's ship do not seem to have been sadistic or cruel. The usual practice was to require only one-third of the *forsairs* to row at a time, except in emergency. Knox was in his prime at thirty-three years of age and, apart from one severe bout of illness, seems to have survived well. He was not the kind of man who would have attracted attention, either by cringing or by provoking the *comite* through truculence. The strong will and spirit he evidenced throughout the rest of his life would have served him well for the ordeal. Above all, he and the Castilians had their Christian faith, and the parallels with St Paul's voyages and imprisonments would no doubt not have been lost on them.

One interesting illustration of the apparent tolerance of the *comite* emerges from Knox's *History* [I, 108]. He was rather ironically billeted in a galley with the name of *Nostre Dame*, which had gone round Brittany to winter at Nantes at the mouth of the Loire. Mass was taking place and after the Salve Regina was sung, a little statue of Our Lady was brought round for kissing. Knox would have none of it but it was thrust in his face. He waited until no one was looking and threw the statue overboard, declaring, 'Now let our lady save herself; she is light enough, let her learn to swim!' He wrote with relish that there were no more attempts to force them to submit to idolatry after that.

Another incident which illustrates that the regimen of galley life was not that of a concentration camp is that he was brought a manuscript Balnaves had written in Mont St Michel on the subject of justification. Despite lying in irons at Rouen, 'sore troubled by corporal infirmitie', he managed to divide it into chapters, make a summary and annotate it in the margin for unlearned readers as well as add an exhortatory letter of his own to the Congregation at St Andrews. The documents were sent, presumably with the help of the thriving Scottish community along the French coast, many of whom were active Protestants.

This network of communications within the Protestant movement was also used in 1555 when Robert Norvell, a Scots Protestant prisoner in the Bastille, succeeded in smuggling out his book *Mirror of a Christian* which was subsequently published in Edinburgh.

On another occasion Knox received a letter from Kirkcaldy of Grange's son William and a group of other young lairds at Mont St Michel, asking if he thought they were justified in escaping. William's father (the man who stabbed the innocent castle porter at St Andrews) was held prisoner at Cherbourg and had already advised him not to escape, since it would possibly result in reprisals on the other Scottish prisoners. Knox told the young man he should not worry about reprisals since such fear came from love of self. He told him he should go ahead and try to escape, but that he should not kill any innocent guard in the process. Knox makes an interesting distinction between killing Beaton (a righteous act) and killing an innocent man (which came under the prohibition of the fifth commandment). We will look later at how far Knox's thinking evolved through his twenty active years (ch. 17), but there is no doubt that his experience in the galleys was influential. As Ridley contends, not even for the sake of Protestant propaganda was he prepared to let the world know about his sufferings: 'Knox did not want martyrdom; he wanted victory.'

Victory was still a long way off in the winter of 1547-8. Although the English government had been making strenuous efforts to obtain the release of the prisoners, the Castilians were not their principal concern. A number of English advisers had travelled back to St Andrews with Henry Balnaves in the spring of 1547 and had been taken prisoner by Strozzi along with the Scots. Since England and France were not at war, the English government argued that they were being detained illegally.

Although France was not actually at war with England, Henry II had stepped up the level of military assistance to Scotland. By June 6 6,000 French troops were ashore in Scotland. A council had been held to consider the removal of the Queen to France, and in January 1548 Mary of Guise managed to get Arran to sign an agreement with the French king, which was ratified by the Scottish Parliament in July. One of the inducements was that Arran would receive a French dukedom, that of Chatelherault in the Loire valley. Although the title he assumed was not that of a full *duc*, his role in Scottish history is not without a monument. Near the Hamilton family home, above the town of Hamilton, a hunting lodge was built on the model of the grand façades of the Loire. Now a museum, it stands high on the hill to the west of the M74 motorway, as a parable of the career of one of Scotland's most ineffective leaders – impressive in the distance but on closer inspection discovered to be mostly façade.

By one of those quirks of fate that would stretch credibility if it appeared in fiction, Knox's galley was off the east coast of Scotland in the summer of 1548. He might easily have watched other French ships emerge from the port of Leith and turn, not to France but towards the north of Scotland. They were on their way round to Scotland's west coast to the fortress of Dumbarton Rock, where the Queen was waiting to be taken to France. Knox and Mary Queen of Scots were not to meet for another thirteen years, when their destinies would then collide, head on.

Knox sometimes writes in retrospect as if he prophesied events, as he did when writing of the summer he fell ill in the galley. It was thought he was not going to live. James Balfour, who sat near him, probably in an effort to keep his spirits up shook him and asked if he recognised the spires he could see through the porthole. 'Yes,' said Knox:

> I know it well for I see the steeple of that place where God first in public opened my mouth to his glory and I am fully persuaded that how weak I now appear, that I shall not depart this life till that my tongue shall glorify his godly name in that same place.

They were lying off Fife, and could see St Andrews. Whether or not he did in fact say these words at the time, he lived to see them come true. For reasons that he does not reveal, Knox and Alexander Clark were released at the beginning of 1549. Around the same time, Kirkcaldy's son and his companions escaped from Mont St Michel – without killing anyone. They got their guards drunk on the feast of the Epiphany and slipped away. Knox got a reward from the English government and the chance to take up a new appointment – as a preacher. This time he did not hesitate to seize the opportunity.

6

Turbulent Preacher

The most likely reason for Knox's release from the galleys was the intercession of the English government. When he reached England with Alexander Clark in March 1549, Knox was given a reward of £5 – about the same for his stint of nineteen months as he would have earned as an unskilled labourer. The escapees from Mont St Michel arrived in England some weeks later and contacted Knox and Clark. The others were not so lucky for they had to wait until July the following year for their release. Mary of Guise and her brother Charles, Cardinal of Lorraine, persuaded the French king to release the rest of the lairds, who were allowed to return to Scotland and were restored to their lands and offices. The Dowager Queen Mary's leniency can be directly attributed to her exasperation with the Earl of Arran. Strengthened by the French forces now in Scotland, she was actively pursuing a policy of rapprochement with the Protestants in order to undermine Arran's position.

So why did Knox not return to Scotland? Why did he prefer to accept the offer of a post as preacher in England? The answer usually given is that the toleration of Protestants had not yet commenced in his native land when he was offered the post of preacher at Berwick in 1549. It would not have been safe for him to go home, since he could still have been tried for treason as a Castilian or as a heretic for his Protestant ideas, but Knox was close enough to Lothian to keep in contact with events in Scotland. The border town of Berwick was full of Scottish emigrants, many of them illegal. The simplest explanation of his reluctance to return may be that Knox found England a more attractive prospect and chose deliberately to remain there.

However he soon found that if Scotland was divided against itself, so too was England. The Lord Protector, the Duke of Somerset, was uncle to the twelve-year-old King Edward and along with the Archbishop of Canterbury, Cranmer, was committed to religious reform. However it had by no means been determined what path this ought to take. The Swiss Protestants had evolved a system of 'civil theocracy' in which church and state were two inseparable faces of the same divinely-minted coin, and in which the magistrate played a central role through a system of civil and ecclesiastical courts. In Germany the Lutherans had adhered to the Catholic system of a clerical hierarchy which ran the church, but this was in turn subject to the prince or king, whose authority came from God. The English Reformation had changed little in the Catholic form of service or system of church government but had transferred the powers vested in the pope to the monarch. There was an internal battle going on between the 'internationalists', who were committed to Swiss and German ideas, led by men like Bishop John Hooper, and the more conservative and establishment-minded wing surrounding Protector Somerset, which can be described as the 'English school'. The latter included William Cecil, the Bishop of London (Nicholas Ridley) and Cranmer himself. Undermining the efforts of both were first the Catholics, many of whom had become nominal Anglicans under Henry VIII and were still hoping for a reversal of their fortunes. There was also a radical group in England, many of whom had arrived there as refugees. They were the Anabaptists, and were feared by both the Reformers and the Catholics because of their appetite for revolution and their potential influence among the lower classes. Neither the Reformers nor the Catholics wanted a repetition in England of the 1525 Peasants' Revolt in Germany, in which Thomas Muntzer, an Anabaptist, had led a revolution which would have established a form of fundamentalist rule that would have proved equally hostile to both.

It was unlikely that Knox would take kindly to the guidelines for preachers which Somerset had issued the previous year:

> It is not the preacher's part to bring that into contempt and hatred which the prince doth either allow, or is content to suffer . . . It is the part of a godly man not to think himself wiser than the King's Majesty or Council, but patiently to expect and conform himself.

This was a quite different form of protestantism from that which Wishart had preached. It expected the church to conform to the state and those within the church to be subject to their bishops. Knox's diocesan bishop at Berwick was the seventy-five-year-old Bishop of Durham, Cuthbert Tunstall, former friend of Erasmus and Sir Thomas More, and not in sympathy with Protestant ideas. As Bishop of London under Henry VIII, Tunstall had suppressed English Bibles and Lutheran pamphlets, and had opposed every reform Cranmer had introduced. It did not bode well.

As a Lowland Scot, Knox spoke a different language from the English and we have evidence that he changed his speech and adopted English forms. When he finally returned to Scotland a decade later the Scots content increased – perhaps in response to the gibes which were made about his English mode of speech – and some of his letters and sermons contain Scotticisms. It was as if a preacher from the deep south in America found himself in Washington or Boston: his speech would have been quaint but not risible and would even have enhanced the impact of his utterances. Because so much of Knox's work was transcribed it is not certain how many of the Scotticisms were added or subtracted by scribes, but there is enough evidence to show that, although bilingual in Scots and English, he chose to use the latter [Murison, in Shaw pp. 40f]. (Arguably that decision had repercussions for the production of a Bible in Scots and was thus one of the main factors in the death of the Scots tongue.)

Certainly from 1550 Knox's writing is entirely in English and the pressure would have been on him to keep it that way. The Scots were not popular in England but were perceived as perfidious allies of the French. The English soldiers who made up the garrison at Berwick were accustomed to killing Scots as their enemy and to viewing with contempt the emigrants who acted as collaborators, and who assisted them on brutal forays into Scottish territory. It is a tribute to Knox's ability as a preacher that he managed to build up a following among Scots emigrants and English soldiers. Berwick in the 1550s was a wild and woolly border town with a population of 3,500 closely confined in squalid conditions. It possessed a parish church that could not possibly seat them all. Knox's lessons in life at the castle of St Andrews and in the French galleys had clearly suited him to this new environment. His robust sermons were the centrepiece of his services. He disliked traditional liturgy, indeed he once described the English Prayer Book as a 'mingle-mangle'. In the north of England Roman catholicism was still strong and this gave Knox extra fuel for his fire as a preacher, inveighing against the mass as idolatry. Within a year of going to Berwick his activities brought him to the attention of the Bishop of Durham, whose views were decidedly High Church. On April 4 1550 Knox was summoned to explain his attacks to the Council of the North at a meeting in a Newcastle church, which included several prominent Catholic nobles.

A major controversy, not simply among Protestants and Catholics but among Protestants in Europe, for the past generation had concerned Holy Communion. Was there a Real Presence in the bread and wine or a spiritual presence, or was the service a memorial of what Christ had done at the Last Supper? The Pope, Henry VIII, Bishop Tunstall and Luther were all agreed in supporting the Real Presence. Luther and the Zurich reformer Ulrich Zwingli quarrelled bitterly over the issue and this caused a division between the German and Swiss Reformation which was to become permanent. Calvin adopted a middle way which held that the bread and wine accompanied the spiritual presence and true body of Christ, a position sometimes called 'consubstantiation'.

Knox was to follow Calvin broadly but his concern was with form rather than doctrine, with systems in conflict rather than the individuals who might be part of them. Knox talked about 'the mass' rather than the sacrament of the altar or the Real Presence. He concentrated on practice which he saw as idolatrous. This distinction fits in with the pattern of his personality as a man of action more than a thinker who belonged

to a particular school. This approach emerged in his defence
to the council, which he later published. In scholastic fashion
he based his argument on a syllogism. First, that all worshipping
of God invented by man without divine command (or to which
is added a wicked opinion) is idolatry. Second, the mass was
invented by man and consists of a wicked opinion. Thus, he
concluded, the mass is idolatry. The wicked opinion was that
Christ's sacrifice could be repeated by a priest saying words.
It was as vain, said Knox, as putting a small piece of sticking-
plaster on a gaping wound.

Here is the kernel of Knox's doctrine on sacraments and
church practices, namely, that nothing should be permitted that
could not be justified from Scripture. But it is only when he
gets past the syllogisms that we see the vintage Knox emerging
and get a taste of the quality of preaching which made his
reputation. The crushing invective, not without a touch of ironic
humour, is devastatingly applied to those who use masses to
achieve various good causes, such as peace in times of war or
even fair weather:

> Vain trifles profane the sacrament . . . should it not then
> be used to pray that toothache be taken away from us or
> oxen should not take ill? . . . In the papistical Mass the
> congregation getteth nothing except the beholding of your
> duckings, noddings, crossings, turning, uplifting, which are
> all but a diabolical profanation of Christ's Supper. Now duck,
> nod, cross as ye list – they are nothing but your own
> inventions!

He goes on to deal with the fact that the congregation at mass
is not necessarily required to receive bread and wine physically,
but can, by virtue of being spectators, participate spiritually.
Christ, he says, did not institute the sacrament so that people
should duck, bow and cross themselves as spectators but that
they should eat and drink: 'What comfort have these men taken
from us,' he exclaims, 'that the sight of it should be considered
sufficient!'

There is a postscript which reveals Knox's thinking on the
question of sacraments:

I will observe that where I say there resteth no sacrifice nor yet is there any priests, I mean any priests having power to offer such oblations. Otherwise I do know that all true Christians are kings and priests and do daily offer unto God a sacrifice most acceptable: the mortification of their affections.

He finished, as in his first sermon at St Andrews, with a challenge to prove that anything he had said was not contained in Scripture. Knox's defence had rested on the three classic Protestant doctrines: the primacy of Scripture (over church traditions and canon law); justification by faith alone; and the priesthood of all believers. However, tactfully, he did not draw out (as he had at St Andrews) the moral of the first doctrine, namely that Scripture took precedence over the power of a Lord Protector or an archbishop's Prayer Book in matters of religious practice.

Bishop Tunstall realised that if he took any action against Knox, the preacher would probably attract support from London for his views on the Real Presence, and he was anxious to keep things the way they were in the north. Knox was allowed to return to Berwick from Newcastle, with his fame considerably enhanced by the episode. Instead it was Tunstall who departed the scene, in the coup mounted in the autumn of 1550, when the Earl of Warwick deposed Somerset and made himself Lord Protector, taking the title of Duke of Northumberland a year later. Somerset's policies in Scotland had resulted in driving the Scots into the arms of the French and at home he had been discredited by the Catholic rising in Cornwall and an agrarian revolt in the east. His sympathy for peasant farmers was regarded as encouraging the peasants' revolt which they all feared. Warwick may have backed the Catholics but his watchword was expediency. He concluded a defeatist treaty with France ('Now you have eaten the cabbages,' he told the French ambassador, 'I suppose you want the garden'). He also backed the landlords against their tenants with the result that land enclosures were enforced, and decided that the Protestants could be used to help asset-strip the property and income of the church. Bishop Tunstall was imprisoned not merely because he was of the *ancien régime*, but because the new Protector had his eyes on half the diocese of Durham and introduced a bill to deprive Tunstall of his see (to Cranmer's outrage).

England now had a Reformed Church, but as it was under the control of the state and the leaders of the state were less than godly, the church was thus tarnished. Although the more radical Protestant wing enjoyed the new Protector's favour and he ingratiated himself with them by forbidding King Edward's half-sister, Princess Mary, to have masses said at her house, they were soon to become suspicious of Warwick's motives. However the radical Protestants were careful to mute their criticism of the vices of the nobles, since if they fell from power, Catholic nobles were waiting in the wings to re-establish their religion. For instance, it would not have been expedient for Knox to have pointed out that, while gambling was illegal, the Warden of the Eastern Marches, Lord Rutland, had run up huge gaming debts, which were paid out of funds which would otherwise have gone to build a much-needed new bridge over the Tweed at Berwick and a far bigger parish church.

At all events, Knox seems to have been very happy with his situation. He must have been well aware that in Scotland Mary of Guise's feud with Arran had improved matters for the Protestants and that the Castilian lairds had finally got back their lands. So why did he not go back to Scotland? The answer can be found in his congregation at Berwick. But was it young Marjory Bowes or her mother Elizabeth who had the greater pull over his heart?

IOANNES CNOXVS.

Above: Portrait of John Knox, published in Beza's *Icones* in 1580.

Left: Plan of St Andrews by John Geddy, c. 1580, showing the Cathedral centre right and the Castle at the top.

IEAN CNOX, DE GIFFORD
EN ESCOSSE.

Above: Portrait of John Knox which appeared in *Les vrais pourtraits des hommes illustres,* published in 1581 (thought also to be of William Tyndale).

Right: A page from Knox's *The First Blast of the Trumpet,* published in Geneva in 1558.

THE FIRST BLAST
TO AWAKE WOMEN
degenerate.

T O promote a woman to beare rule, superióritie, dominion or empire aboue any realme, nation, or citie, is repugnāt to nature, cōtumelie to God, a thing moſt contrarious to his reueled will and approued ordināce, and finallie it is the ſubuerſion of good order, of all equitie and iuſtice.

In the probation of this propoſition, I will not be ſo curious, as to gather what ſoeuer may amplifie, ſet furth, or decore the ſame, but I am purpoſed, euen as I haue ſpoken my conſcience in moſt plaine ād fewe wordes, ſo to ſtād content with a ſimple proofe of euerie membre, bringing in for my witneſſe Goddes ordinance in nature, his plaine will reueled in his worde, and the mindes of ſuch as be moſte auncient amongeſt godlie writers.

And firſt, where that I affirme the em-

B 1

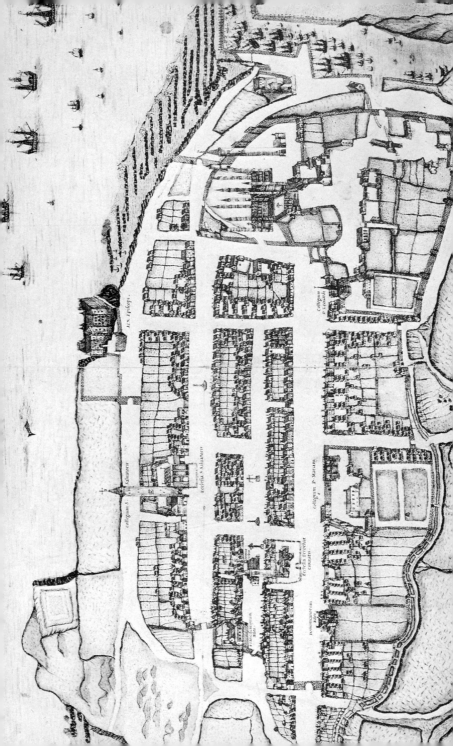

Arx Apilogis.

collegium S. Adriatorii

Ecclesia S Adriatorii

Collegium et Leatioli

collegium D. Mariani

Ecclesia remediae Civitatis

SEPULCHRITUR
REX

DOMINI CANTORUM

7

The Ladies' Man

Knox's relationships with women and particularly Mrs Bowes make a fascinating study. His detractors have made all kinds of accusations that he committed adultery with the mother and married the daughter to keep up a respectable front. Some Protestant scholars have seen the relationship as a friendship, others a pastoral dependency which was primarily spiritual. They point out that it was common for respectable Protestant women who no longer had recourse to the confessional to consult preachers. Yes, we might add, but not to abandon their husbands and go abroad to live with the preachers!

Elizabeth Bowes was no ordinary woman. She was the daughter and co-heir of Sir Roger Aske of Yorkshire and married to Richard Bowes, whose lands were at Dalden near Durham but who had been appointed captain of Norham Castle near Berwick, the largest of the fortresses in the English bulwark against Scotland. They had been married nearly thirty years and she had borne him fifteen children, of whom ten were daughters. The fifth, Marjory, was with her at Norham and when they went seven miles to Berwick to hear Knox preach, they both fell under his spell. Not only was it a formidable assertion of marital independence in those times to adopt a different religion in public, but to become a Protestant in the predominantly Catholic north marks Elizabeth Bowes as a decidedly liberated lady. Jasper Ridley rather unkindly says of her that a woman of forty-five who has had fifteen confinements is unlikely to have retained her sexual attractions, but this could prove the opposite.

The *ménage à trois* which began at Berwick continued throughout Knox's stay in Geneva and finally, on his return to Scotland, played an important part in his life. It is extremely relevant as a key to his complex character.

It is a fact well known to clergymen of all faiths that some middle-aged women develop a 'crush' on their minister or priest. It is silly to pretend in the post-Freudian age that these feelings do not have a sexual component. The inter-personal chemistry, tension, attraction – whatever we call it – often retains its magic all the more for never gaining physical expression. On the man's part, the woman of a 'certain age' can be variously a mother-figure, a sublimated sexual fantasy or simply a feminine presence which the male-dominated world of the clergy profoundly lacks. The fact that Mrs Bowes lived with her daughter and Knox does not negate any of the above. One does not have to choose between adultery and spirituality to make sense of their relationship. It was a close friendship, cemented by an exchange of letters over a decade. Twenty-seven of those letters have survived, preserved by Mrs Bowes and passed to Knox's manservant, Richard Bannatyne, who had them transcribed, possibly with some editing. Only one letter from Knox to Marjory Bowes survives among them, which he coyly signs, 'I think that this be the first letter that ever I wrote you,' and so the picture is far from complete. However without these letters we would lack insights into the more tender and much more humane side of Knox than is revealed in the combative tracts written for public consumption, or the caustic commentary, *History of the Reformation*, written when he had been pushed out of the picture.

Extracts from the letters give a perspective on this friendship (later to be paralleled by Knox's attachment to Mrs Anne Locke, the wife of a London Protestant merchant who came out to Geneva to join his family for a period later in the decade). The thrust of many of Knox's letters to Mrs Bowes was her 'troubled conscience' and after her death, when he was extremely wearied of life, he writes [*Works*, VI, 481ff] that the reason for their great familiarity was simply her over-active conscience and not flesh and blood. This somewhat ungallant dismissal has been taken by some of his supporters to be evidence that he found her obsessive self-doubt wearisome, but it should be read against the context of melancholia in which he wrote at the time. The magic was all gone and Knox was having to defend himself against innuendoes about their relationship and thus played it down. His actions and letters over a longer period tell of a deeper involvement. From the time of his betrothal to her daughter, Knox addresses Mrs Bowes as 'dearly beloved mother'. One senses in Mrs Bowes an intensity that might border at times on the neurotic but would have made Knox feel that he was special. The country boy from Lothian who was plucked from his tutoring to endure a ghastly year and a half in the galleys was now being made to feel important and special by this attractive woman from the upper classes. She boosted his confidence, psychologically and sexually. But let the letters speak for themselves.

Knox wrote about their relationship:

Since the very first day that it pleased the providence of God to bring you and me in familiarity, I have always delighted in your company and when labours would permit you know I have not spared hours to talk and commune with you the fruit whereof I did not then fully understand or perceive. But now absent and so absent that by corporal presence neither of us can receive comfort of other, I call to mind that oftimes when with dolorous hearts we have begun our talking, God hath sent great comfort unto both, which now for my own part I commonly want. The exposition of your troubles and acknowledging of your infirmity was first unto me a very mirror and glass wherein I beheld myself so rightly painted forth that nothing could be more evident to my own eyes . . . judge not, mother, that I write these things debasing myself other than I am – nay, I am worse than my pen can express. In body you think I am no adulterer; let so be, but the heart is infected with foul lusts and will albeit I lament never same kill. Externally I commit no adultery but my wicked heart lusts itself and cannot be restrained from vain imaginings.

Those who accuse Knox of being a bully or a brute are forced to come to terms in these letters with a pastor who combines sensitivity to the anxieties of others with an appreciation of his own faults and shortcomings. His letter to Marjory reads more like a sermon but includes the line, 'The spirit of God shall instruct your heart what is most comfortable to the troubled conscience of your mother, and pray earnestly that so may be.' The fact that Knox wrote his wife letters with so much theological and pastoral content should not be taken to indicate that he dealt with his nearest and dearest as if they were parishioners to be preached at. The fashion to write in such godly terms persisted beyond the sixteenth century.

Regarding this one extant letter to Marjory, it has been concluded by some that it demonstrates that he was much more interested in the mother than the daughter. But equally it could suggest that other letters to Marjory were too personal to be handed to a secretary for safe keeping. She may have destroyed them herself. Knox's letters to Mrs Bowes were presumably left behind in the custody of Richard Bannatyne when she left the household after Marjory's death. It was inevitable that because of his public notoriety any of Knox's private relationships would be the subject of much prurient interest, as indeed they were. Accusations of impropriety in his relationship with Mrs Bowes were present from the beginning and did not cease with his death.

Over three hundred years later R. L. Stevenson wrote an essay on the relationship of Knox to women [*Men & Books*, 1895], in which he suggests that the marriage to Marjory was a device got up by Mrs Bowes to stop the tongues wagging, while at the same time enabling her to remain close to Knox [p. 375]. Stevenson writes:

It cannot be said that Knox's intercourse with women was quite of the highest sort. It is characteristic that we find him more alarmed for his own reputation than for the reputation of the women with whom he was familiar. There was a fatal preponderance of self in all his intimacies; many women came to learn from him, but he never became a learner in return. [p. 393]

But Stevenson almost at once contradicts himself when he concedes [p. 394]:

In the strong quiet patience of all his letters to the weariful Mrs Bowes we may perhaps see one cause of the fascination that he possessed for these religious women. Here was one you could besiege all the year round with inconsistent scruples and complaints . . . and he would read all this patiently and sympathetically and give you an answer in the most reassuring polysyllables like a treatise on divinity. And then those easy tears of his . . . here was this great-voiced man of God who might be seen beating the solid pulpit every Sunday . . . and who on Monday would sit with them in their parlours and weep with them over their manifold trials and tribulations.

It seems here that Stevenson (who in his own correspondence often bewailed the lack of feminine company in his life) wants it both ways. He criticises Knox for not learning from women yet admits the Reformer showed great patience in his dealings with those who consulted him. He concludes that Knox was kind to women in his own way, 'not the worst way, even if it was not the best way – and once at least, if not twice moved to his heart of hearts by a woman'. Knox remained loyal to his circle of women, and, considering the burden of stress he was under at times in his life, still found time to write to his closest confidants. They also remained loyal to him. When Mrs Bowes seems to think he imagined that her allegiance to the 'cause' was in doubt – when Catholic Queen Mary had gained the throne and he was preparing to flee the country – Knox undertook a dangerous journey north to see mother and daughter, and wrote to reassure Elizabeth:

Dear mother. . . God I take to record in my conscience that (there is) none this day within the realm of England with whom I would more gladly speak (only she whom God had offered unto me and has commanded me to love as my own flesh except) than with you.

This does not have the ring of a man who simply accepted an arranged marriage as a means of making respectable his relationship to her mother, but a genuinely caring person.
Captain Bowes, not surprisingly, was less impressed by Knox.

He was a Catholic and his job was to command soldiers against the Scots. Knox was a lower-class renegade priest and even if the marriages of former priests had become legal in 1549, they were certainly not considered respectable. Bowes seems to have had no suspicions that the preacher's relationship with his wife was in any way dishonourable. There is no record that he objected to the handfasting of Knox and Marjory, a north country custom which was the first step to marriage (hence Knox's references to 'wife' and 'mother' prior to the legal marriage). At the time of the betrothal, which was possibly in December 1552, since the 'mother' references begin in January 1553, Knox had risen in favour to become a court preacher to Edward VI and thus would have been more socially acceptable. The age difference was not unusual; Knox was thirty-eight and Marjory twenty years his junior.

But when Knox next came north to pursue his suit in January 1554, when the King was dead and his Roman Catholic half-sister Mary was on the throne, he was no longer a respectable person and certainly someone of Richard Bowes's class and position would have given him short shrift. In Mary's England it was social suicide to ally your family to a radical Scottish preacher. Bowes had two successful brothers, the one Warden of the East and Middle Marches (Sir Robert), and the elder brother, Sir Ralph (knighted after Flodden), and they now closed ranks against Knox. The preacher sought an interview with Sir Robert Bowes to see if he would support his suit, but with the change of government Sir Robert was fighting to hold on to his wardenship and was probably appalled that he might be accused of conspiring with a man whose activities would certainly put him on the list of wanted Protestants that Queen Mary's supporters were preparing. Sir Robert showed Knox the door and also prevented him seeing Marjory or Elizabeth. When the preacher tried to persuade him to change his mind, Bowes angrily said that he would have none of his rhetoric. Knox was hurt by the rejection and the 'disdainful hatred', but it did not stop him pursuing his suit. The marriage eventually took place (in 1555) despite the fact that, initially, he was forced to leave England without Marjory or Elizabeth Bowes.

During this period he wrote several letters to Mrs Bowes and it is quite clear that neither Knox nor mother and daughter had any intention of letting the matter drop, dangerous as it might be for all of them.

The question still remains, were Knox and Elizabeth Bowes lovers? The rumours about Mrs Bowes and Knox were current in the winter of 1551-2 and twice he refers to them in letters to her. Then in February 1552 he writes:

Call to your mind what I did standing at the cupboard in Alnwick; in very deed I thought that no creature had been tempted as I was. And when I heard proceed from your mouth the very same words that he troubles me with, I did wonder, and from my heart lament your sair trouble, knowing in myself the dolour thereof . . .

These words do seem to suggest physical intimacy and perhaps Knox had previously touched or embraced Mrs Bowes. But there it seems to have ended. It is unlikely that the marriage with Marjory could have survived, as it clearly did, if the *ménage à trois* had been less than innocent. It was a happy marriage and Marjory is twice referred to by Calvin in glowing terms when she died: 'whose like is not to be found everywhere' (to Knox); and 'most delightful of wives' (to Goodman). She was not only his 'dear bedfellow' but acted as his secretary on occasion and her death devastated him. Nor was Mrs Bowes cast aside. Not only did she live with them in Geneva and Edinburgh, but following Marjory's death in 1560 and her return to England, Knox asked her to come back in 1562 to look after his two young sons, which she did until he remarried in 1564.

Knox refers to Mrs Bowes having died in a letter of 1572. Two of her sons figure further in the Anglo-Scottish saga, one as Warden of Berwick (Sir George), the other as English ambassador to Scotland (Sir Robert). Neither Elizabeth nor Marjory was even mentioned in her husband, Richard Bowess', will, a bitter consequence of their decision to follow the Scots preacher.

8

Black Rubric

That Knox had charisma as a preacher is not usually disputed.
His preaching was having such an effect in Berwick that it was
actually attracting more emigrants over the border from Scotland.
When Knox began taking services further south, in Newcastle,
in the summer of 1551, many of the Scots moved with him. There
are no records of trouble from them but the authorities were wary
of this phalanx of Scots infiltrating their country.

When an outbreak of sweating sickness hit England in August
1551, Knox saw it as a punishment for the sins of the nobles in
not implementing the virtues of their religion. This message must
have had great appeal to good-living artisans and merchants, who
were forced to regard such people as their superiors in a class-
ridden society. He took a bolder step when the Lord Protector,
who had now taken the title of Duke of Northumberland, began
to rule with a heavier hand. Charges of sedition became more
common than under Henry VIII and one of the targeted victims
was the former Protector Somerset, the man who had brought
Knox to England. Without naming Lord Protector
Northumberland straight out, Knox said that it was a gleeful
conspiracy by Roman Catholic nobles to set one champion of
protestantism to destroy the other and if Somerset died then it
would be the ruin of his adversary. He did and it was, but not
before Northumberland had tried to appease Cranmer's
nationalistic Anglicans with the promise that they might now
prepare their own Prayer Book. When Northumberland arrived
in the north in June 1552 ready to carve up the Durham diocese

from which Tunstall had been removed, Knox's sermons were scaling new heights of controversy. The preacher later wrote that in his sermons he pulled no punches about what would happen if the present scale of corruption in high places continued. But far from alienating Northumberland, Knox seems to have impressed him, for after talking together the Lord Protector took Knox back to London with him and appointed him a court preacher. This strange development requires some explanation, which Knox himself does not offer.

The character of Northumberland, a harsh man of the world, does not easily fit him to be an admirer of Knox. Perhaps there was something in him of the hard-headed businessman, fascinated by ideals that he knows he can never attain; but this seems unlikely. The explanation most historians offer is that he felt he could use Knox and the radical Protestants to help him dismantle the Roman Catholic Church's patrimony and keep at arm's length those within the established Church of England who might want their share of it. Northumberland had already offered the leading radical, Hooper, the new, enlarged bishopric of Worcester and Gloucester (in return for creaming off most of the income) and Hooper had agreed. Northumberland probably thought that every man had his price and assumed that the fiery Scot could be bought off in the same way. He thought he could use Knox against Cranmer, who had been causing trouble over the Tunstall affair. This explanation also does justice to the backing Knox got when he attacked the new Prayer Book in one of his first sermons at court.

Cranmer's Prayer Book, at first sight, was something that might have appealed to Knox, since it abolished many vestments and contained words which were hardly compatible with the Real Presence. The new edition was to come into force on All Saints day (November 1) 1552 and was to be the only form of service permitted in the Church of England. Knox was used to being able to exercise discretion in the choice of the order of his service, and when he read that kneeling to receive communion was to become the norm, he disliked it a lot. Did this not smell of the kind of idolatry that was directed towards the mass? If sitting was good enough for Jesus, was it not good enough for others? The date of the sermon in which Knox voices these objections is generally thought to have been September at Windsor with the new book already at the printer's. The Privy Council backed Knox (whose views were shared by the others on the radical wing), and asked Cranmer and Ridley to reconsider kneeling as part of the rubric. Cranmer replied on October 7 that of course Christ did not kneel, but if they followed the custom of the time they would eat lying on the ground as the Turks and Tartars still did. He urged the council to pay no attention to 'these glorious and unquiet spirits, which can like nothing but that is after their own fancy, and cease not to make trouble and disquietness when things be quiet and in good order'. In other words, don't allow this fellow to rock the boat.

However, the council did not entirely side with the Archbishop. Knox and his radical colleagues were asked to comment on the Forty-five Articles of Faith drawn up by Cranmer (which eventually became forty-two and later, under Elizabeth, the Thirty-Nine Articles, which are the basis of the Church of England confession). The bulk of the Cranmer Prayer Book was common ground between them, but they redoubled their criticism of the kneeling clause. It was not a trivial matter to them. They argued as follows: kneeling implied adoration; it would give papists the chance to say there was no difference between their mass and the Anglican communion; Christ sat at his supper; finally, sitting was a sign of joy. The Privy Council then asked Cranmer to prepare a statement to be incorporated into the new Prayer Book which emphasised that kneeling was not superstitious adoration but simply reverence. This was printed on a separate sheet and pasted into the copies already printed, which became known as the Black Rubric. It stated that the fact that communicants were to receive on their knees did not imply adoration of the elements, as Christ was not really present in the bread and wine since he was in heaven and could not be in two places at the same time.

On the surface it seemed a victory for Knox, but it was actually a victory for Cranmer. The Prayer Book remained unamended and kneeling was now the norm. Knox had to conform, and we see his pragmatic side in the way he dealt with the consequences. He wrote a long, face-saving letter to his congregation in Berwick, which is important because it reveals how far he was prepared to go at that time in conforming to the English pattern of state religion and to the views on obedience to secular authority, which he was to revise radically:

> Remembering always, beloved brethren, that due obedience be given to magistrates, rulers and princes, without tumult, grudge or sedition; for how wicked that ever themselves be in life, as how ungodly that ever their precepts or commandments be, ye must obey them for conscience sake; except in chief points of religion; and then ought ye to obey God not man; not to pretend to defend God's truth or religion (ye being subjects) by violence or sword, but patiently suffering what God shall please be laid upon you for constant confession of your faith and belief.

This is a different Knox from the man who was giving communion to the Castilians; and from the man who was to flee England just over a year later. He went on in his letter to point out that he neither repented of nor recanted his former stance on the matter and had been reassured by the insertion of the Black Rubric, by the admission of the authorities that kneeling was a human invention, and by the fact that he had not been condemned for what he had done previously. He was not telling them to conform because of fear of reprisals but because of good order and obedience to authority. This letter, which is not included in Knox's *Works*, has the hollow feel of self-justification.

Knox the preacher was learning to become a politician. The strains of acting out of character were beginning to tell. There was a recurrence of the poor health he had experienced in the galley. He thought he had found his niche in England, where there was reformed religion and the prospect of a happy marriage, but underneath the tensions were beginning to show.

At the height of the kneeling controversy Northumberland put him under even more pressure by offering him the bishopric of Rochester in Kent, in addition to an *ex gratia* payment of £40. The Protector candidly admitted in a letter to Cecil that his reason for doing this was to kill three birds with one stone: first Knox's presence would undermine Archbishop Cranmer in the diocese of Canterbury, which was adjacent to Rochester; secondly he would be a useful hammer of the Anabaptist faction which was strong in Kent; and thirdly his departure for the south would staunch the flow of Scots emigrants who were coming to the Newcastle congregation, attracted by Knox's preaching.

Knox's refusal of the bishopric is a perplexing and much misunderstood action. He did not turn it down because he disapproved of bishops, as some of his more ardent Protestant admirers have alleged. As several scholars have pointed out, there is nothing anywhere in his writings which suggests that he regarded episcopacy as such as unscriptural. It was not incompatible with the radical wing of English protestantism, as Hooper had shown, and there was every opportunity to influence events in a much more effective way. So why did he refuse? The simple answer is that he realised he was being bought and used by someone he had come to view with great suspicion. Knox was quite realistic about the motives and morals of Northumberland's government, as he displays in his comments around this time. Furthermore he was not the kind of man who is easily bribed or flattered into submission. As for playing the 'whetstone' (as the Duke put it) to Cranmer, the thought of replaying the kneeling controversy or some other new quarrel with Cranmer must have filled Knox with dismay. The sophisticated Cranmer had outwitted him over kneeling and had skilfully held on to his position under two changes of ruler. Knox was not an aggressive pighead who craved controversy and so cannot be blamed for wanting to duck out of it on this occasion. He probably had little taste for the power struggles and politics of the royal court and felt much more at home in the north where his supporters (and his heart) lay. It is something of an exaggeration [J. Ridley, p. 117ff] to claim that he turned down the bishopric in order to be close to Scotland, where he always thought his future lay, since he had shown no signs of taking the high road to Scotland when it was possible for him to have done so.

However one meeting of relevance to the Scottish situation took place in London the previous October between Knox and Lord James Stewart, Prior of St Andrews. This meeting was distorted by the Roman Catholic writer Nicol Burne into an absurd conspiracy in which the preacher plotted with Lord James to put the latter on the Scottish throne. But it demonstrates that Knox had formed a respect from an early period for this Catholic nobleman who was to become one of the few figures to emerge from the Scottish Reformation with his integrity intact. Lord James will reappear later, but his entry at this point is a reminder that Knox had not lost his interest in the affairs of Scotland.

In a later letter to Mrs Bowes Knox gives a reason for his refusal of the see of Rochester which sounds plausible: 'Assuredly the foresight of trouble to come. How oft have I said unto you, that the time would come when England would not give me bread.' Knox's sojourn at court would have enabled him to see that the young king – who seems to have had a lively mind and attracted the admiration of the preacher – was dying of consumption. Knox could see clearly what lay ahead if the succession passed to Mary: while Cranmer and the leaders of the church were busy being prelates and preparing Prayer Books, Mary was preparing a list of heretics and holding masses at her home with impunity. People at the time possibly thought his obsession with the threat from catholicism to be over-played, but events were to prove him right.

Northumberland did not take kindly to Knox's refusal when Cecil sent him to see the Lord Protector in his Chelsea home at the beginning of December 1552. 'I love not to have to do with men which be neither grateful nor pleasable,' Northumberland wrote to Cecil after that meeting, and complained that he could easily have courted more popularity if he had not made his duty to the King his priority, obviously referring to some complaint that Knox had made about his way of running things. Knox had made a considerable impact in his first year in England, and eighteen months later, when Cranmer, Ridley and Latimer were arraigned by the triumphant Catholic party, their inquisitor Weston taunted them with the fact that when England was Protestant 'a runagate Scot did take away the adoration and worshipping of Christ in the sacrament, by whose procurement that heresy was put into the last communion book; so much prevailed that one man's authority at the time'. However Knox cannot have upset the Duke too much, since he granted him permission to return to the north. When he got there on December 9, Knox was not a happy man: 'This day I am more vile and of low reputation in my own eyes than I was either that day that my feet was chained in the prison of dolour (the galleys I mean) or yet that day that I was delivered by God's only providence from the same.' His words seem to betray a disgust with the compromises he was being forced to make.

So when he got back to his pulpit there was little in his Christmas sermons about peace and goodwill towards all men. The trumpet blew increasingly shrill warnings about the danger of secret papists in high places: 'They thirsted nothing more than the king's death which their iniquity would procure.' Lord Wharton, Warden of the Marches in succession to Northumberland, brought a complaint against Knox to the Privy Council; and Lord Westmoreland, Sheriff of Durham, ordered him to appear before him the next day on pain of treason, and the Mayor of Newcastle denounced him. But Knox was backed by Northumberland, who rebuked his accusers for their 'greedy accusation' and 'malicious stomach'. The upshot was that Knox was summoned south in February 1553 and the Privy Council told Cranmer to appoint him Vicar of All Hallows Church in Bread Street, in Ridley's diocese. Knox again refused to take the appointment. None the less he was appointed one of the court preachers for the Lent series, to preach before Edward VI in March-April 1553. This puzzling second refusal and the mystifying failure of any compulsion to follow it requires some explanation (which Knox does not reveal). Why did Northumberland agree to let Knox turn down the benefice, apparently letting this rebellious Scot do as he pleased? Why did Knox turn it down?

The answer suggested by some biographers is that he knew that Nicholas Ridley, Bishop of London, was a stickler for the Prayer Book and High Anglican orthodoxy and would have come down on him hard. This scarcely seems plausible in view of Ridley's subsequent opposition to a Catholic monarch and his praise of Knox as a Lenten preacher (see p. 68). There were other radical Protestant congregations in London at the time, such as that of John à Lasco, which the Bishop tolerated. The reason for his refusal might instead be found by asking why Northumberland did not compel him to accept. One possible answer is that there was another use for Knox which was growing in the mind of the Lord Protector. He was well aware of the

King's frailty and had made moves to mend his fences with Mary, who had the strongest claim to the succession, but he knew that this had been of little avail. In fact Northumberland was himself involved in a conspiracy to put Lady Jane Grey on the throne. Her marriage to his son was part of her usefulness. Her claim came through her grandmother, the daughter of Henry VII. It was an ill-fated plot for many reasons, but principally because Northumberland had done nothing to prepare the people for the exclusion of Mary, many of whom did not know she was Catholic, and thus she became the obvious and popular choice against his unpopular and widely-despised government. But in the spring of 1553 he needed to prepare the ground for excluding Mary on grounds of religion, and Knox must have seemed the man to do it. His role as roving preacher might enable him to spread the message more widely. This is not to suggest that Knox was part of the Lady Jane Grey plot, but simply that he would have found it more conducive to his priorities to go around the country stirring up opposition against return to Roman catholicism. The two men thus had a mutual interest, and mutually agreed that Knox did not have to go to All Hallows. We must also reiterate Knox's reasons for refusing Rochester, namely that he felt his days in England were numbered and that he would be better able to decide his future without being tied permanently to the Anglican Church. The answer he gave later to the Privy Council, when summoned to account for his refusal, was that he was willing to serve anywhere but felt he could serve better outside London, and that the Lord Protector had told him to refuse the benefice, which appears to have put an end to the matter. He was given an appointment in Amersham, which he took up after the Lent sermons.

The Lent sermons were explosive. Despite the fact that they were a mixed bunch of churchmen, the court preachers were agreed that there was an acute crisis. Grindal, a future Archbishop of Canterbury, warned of the King's approaching death and of his courtiers' spiritual laxity. Lever and Haddon prophesied plagues as judgments on the nation, and Bradford 'spared not the proudest'. Knox's contribution was to compare the situation of the young King with the Old Testament monarchs David and Hezekiah, who were deceived by traitorous counsellors. In his

written account of the sermon he even goes as far as to identify
the 'traitors'. William Paulet, the Treasurer, who was said to
have survived several changes of regime in England because he
was of 'willow, not of oak', was compared to Shebna the 'crafty
fox'. Ridley, writing later from prison while awaiting martyrdom,
wrote of the preachers: 'As for Latimer, Lever, Bradford and
Knox, their tongues were so sharp they ripped in so deep in their
galled backs to have purged them no doubt of the filthy matter
that was festered in their hearts.' Northumberland was not
impressed with this display and appears to have decided that if
the church was not able to be counted on he would do better to
bully it as Henry VIII had done. Cranmer took the brunt of his
assault in the House of Lords and was forced to accept defeat
over changes to canon law which would have given the church
greater independence. Meanwhile the Privy Council had packed
Knox off to Amersham in Buckinghamshire, where he was giving
out dire warnings about the future when the news came that
Edward VI had died on July 6 1553.

The next few months were painful in English history. Within
days the Jane Grey plot failed dismally. Although Ridley spoke
up for her he was howled down. Cranmer had signed for Lady
Jane only under instruction from the dying King, and the general
opinion was that Mary had the right of succession, and the leading
Anglicans' doctrine of Christian obedience prevented them from
standing against it, even although they were well aware of Mary's
devotion to catholicism. Even Hooper was active in Mary's
support. Not so Knox. In the Amersham pulpit during the critical
week in July when the issue had yet to be decided, he thundered:

> O England, England if thou obstinately wilt return unto Egypt;
> that is if thou contract marriage, confederacy or league with
> such princes as do maintain and advance idolatry (such as the
> Emperor, which is no less enemy unto Christ than ever was
> Nero) . . . then assuredly, O England, thou shalt be plagued
> and brought to desolation!

He was referring to the proposed marriage between Mary and
Philip of Spain, son of the Emperor Charles V, and his
comparison of the latter to Nero was as pungent an insult as could

be imagined to a foreign head of state. We should remind ourselves here that in those times any expressions of dissent against monarchs were taken seriously, and that, although there was a protest from the Emperor's ambassadors on July 27 that 'several preachers, certain Scotsmen in particular, have preached scandalous things of late to rouse up the people', Knox was lucky to escape and find himself still able to preach in London, since initially Mary moved only against Northumberland and his family. In retrospect we can see that what Knox had warned against all along soon came to pass. While the religious wars of Europe see-sawed, in England the Reform movement suffered a huge setback and seemed about to be subsumed under the Catholic monarchies of Europe.

On August 12 Mary announced that she intended to remain Catholic but would not compel adherence to her faith. However she prohibited the use of terms such as papist or heretic and forbade anyone to preach without a special licence from the Queen. Up to this point Knox had been showing anguished signs in the material he had written, which, without specifically naming the Queen, suggest that he was trying to reach an accommodation with the new regime. By the autumn he must have realised that this was futile. Mary put Cranmer and Latimer in the Tower in September. She also expelled the congregations of refugee Protestants, and because of the resentment and xenophobia they aroused this was seen as a popular act. Knox knew that he would soon be faced with the choice of flight or the flames, and he chose to flee.

The English Protestants, who taught the duty of obedience to the sovereign in all matters, were easily brought to prison. They were cited to appear and did so. Knox's attitude was about to undergo a sea-change from his call to obedience in the letter to his Berwick congregation on kneeling to receive communion. From now on he seemed to act as if the duty to obey was no longer binding and his conduct at this point sometimes attracts the charge of cowardice. In this he was his own worst enemy, since he devoted much space in letters defending himself against the charge of running away. He no doubt felt that the uncompromising attitude of many members of his congregation put him to shame, and wanted to justify his stance. He was not the first or last leader of a movement to cut and run in order to fight another day. In eight years he would not have forgotten Wishart's fateful words, 'One is enough for a sacrifice.' This time he did not have his 'bairns' to return to, but he did have a prospective 'family' in the persons of Marjory and Elizabeth Bowes and it was not the action of a coward to turn north to try to see them. He wrote to them in advance, but his letters were intercepted. When he arrived in the north in November, it was then that he managed to contact Marjory's uncle, Sir Robert Bowes, but was rebuffed.

Knox knew that it was only a matter of time before he was arrested. He sent Mrs Bowes the first part of his Exposition of the Sixth Psalm, which he had promised to write for her. It is dated January 6 1554 and contains an interesting passage:

> I cannot express the pain which I think I might suffer to have the presence of you, and of others that be like troubled, but a few days. But God shall gather us at his good pleasure; if not in this wretched and miserable life, yet in that state where death may not dissever us. My daily prayer is for the sore afflicted in those quarters. Sometime I have thought that impossible it had been, so to have removed my affection from the realm of Scotland, that any nation or realm could have been equal dear to me. But God I take to record in my conscience that the troubles present (and appearing to be) in the realm of England are double more dolorous unto my heart than ever were the troubles of Scotland.

Here is another pointer that at this juncture Knox's inclinations were not to return to Scotland. During his abortive visit to Sir Robert Bowes it would have been possible for him to have slipped over the border to Scotland, where the Franco-Scottish authorities were not pursuing the Protestants. But he did not do so. His eyes and ambitions were still for England. Controversial as it may be, in January 1554 when Knox landed in Dieppe his heart and his hopes were in England not his native land.

9

Prophet without Honour

Time and again Knox found himself in Dieppe at critical moments of his life. It was at the crossroads of his journeys to and from Europe, and France was the first foreign land on which he had set eyes when he was exiled in the galleys. Yet a Scot in Dieppe was never a stranger in a strange land. There was always a ship leaving for or arriving from Leith or another Scottish port. Today the Rue d'Ecosse, which runs away from the inner harbour, is the memorial to the Scots colony which lived there in the sixteenth century and gave hospitality to Knox. (The taverns of Dieppe would have known the sound of the ballads of the Wedderburn brothers, one of whom made his life among the Huguenots of France.)

We should not think of the French Protestants as similar to any other Protestants in Europe, for they were mainly recruited from the nobility (between two-fifths and a half of the French nobility was at one time Protestant). Save in the south-west, where there is long history of religious dissent, only a minority of peasants became Protestants and the city of Paris and the north-east of France remained Catholic throughout all the religious conflicts. The French Protestants eventually tried to win power by forming themselves into a political party. Although they were the target of persecutions later in the sixteenth century (the worst being the Massacre of St Bartholomew's Eve in 1572), by 1598 they had won equal political rights with Catholics in the Edict of Nantes. Although this far from established 'a free church in a free state', it meant that public office was open to

Huguenots and mixed chambers were established in four important *parlements*. Eventually the Huguenots were crushed as a political party by Richelieu in 1625.

In the days when Knox was travelling through Dieppe, the Huguenots were still a widespread and influential part of French society. This explains how Knox was able to criss-cross France during the next five years without running into trouble. But it was in Dieppe that he spent most of his time. Among his own people there he found inspiration for some of his most controversial writing.

In January 1554 Knox's state of mind seems to have been distraught. Although in future years he does not appear to feel the need to defend himself against the charge of cowardice, in his letters at that time he does. He finally completed his Exposition of the Sixth Psalm and writes to Mrs Bowes:

> Albeit that I have in the beginning of this battle appeared to play the faint-hearted and feeble soldier, yet my prayer is that I may be restored to the battle again . . . England and Scotland shall know that I am ready to suffer more than either poverty or exile, for the profession of that doctrine, and that heavenly religion whereof it has pleased His merciful providence to make me, amongst others, a simple soldier and witness bearer unto men . . .

He adds that there is nothing he would not give for the opportunity to preach a few sermons in England and urges her not to bend with the wind and give in to the pressures to attend mass.

There is a melancholy note in the Exposition, and he finishes his note to Mrs Bowes: 'Seeing it is uncertain, beloved mother, if ever we shall meet in this corporal life, my conscience moveth me to write to you, as though I should take from you my last goodnight on earth.'

Knox has been criticised for being brave from afar, but in his defence it ought to be said that little would have been accomplished had he gone to the stake for a system of religion with which he did not entirely agree and which he was in process of trying to change. It would also have been strange if he had not offered encouragement to those who remained in England and who shared his views. He did not call on them to throw caution to the winds and court martyrdom, but it would have been entirely inconsistent with either his character or his principles if he had advocated 'bowing the knee to Baal' at this stage.

Significantly he does not attack Queen Mary personally but prays that she may be brought to the truth, and focuses the blame on the infidelity of the nobility and the scheming of the leading bishops of the old regime. This may have been a tactic to allow him to return to England if Mary could be persuaded to cease her persecution of Protestants. There is also some disagreement among Knox scholars as to when he actually left England, caused by the dating of his Exposition of the Sixth Psalm. It appears to conflict with the date of a letter written by Calvin referring to the arrival in Geneva of a Scots preacher who had been prominent in England under Edward VI. It seems generally agreed that Knox was the Scot in question. Probably what has happened is that a transcriber has changed the date of 'the very point of my journey' (that is, Dieppe to Geneva) from January 28 to February 28, thus contradicting the date of Calvin's letter (February 23), since Knox could not have arrived in Geneva before leaving Dieppe. This would also explain why he makes no mention of the Wyatt rebellion in Kent which took place in January, and of which he would certainly have had news (or even been implicated in) had he travelled through the south-east of England (his most probable and safest route) any later than January 6. If we accept this explanation [Ridley, pp. 545ff], then Knox left England in early January, remained in Dieppe until the end of the month and still had three weeks to complete a journey across good roads in France, which would normally have taken eleven days at the most.

Knox's travelling expenses would have been met by Protestant merchants in Dieppe who were Scots exiles. He had arrived penniless, not having claimed his £40 stipend which had been due in October. To have done so would have been to risk being thrown in the Tower with Cranmer and the other Protestants rounded up by Queen Mary. It is worth mentioning that at no time does Knox seem to have been short of resources to undertake his journeys. An analysis of the social background of the exiles who made up the English-speaking congregation of which Knox was minister in Geneva shows that a third were gentry (some of whom also numbered among the one-fifth who were students); an eighth were merchants and a sixth artisans, leaving a small number of renegade clerics. This comparatively wealthy group would easily have had the resources to support visiting preachers like Knox.

But his mission in Geneva was not simply to find a job. He came to see Calvin, whose fame was spreading but who was still at this time involved in a power struggle in Geneva. That might explain why Calvin did not initially find much time for Knox and quickly passed him on to his colleagues, Viret in Lausanne and Bullinger in Zurich. Perhaps Calvin was also alarmed at the implications contained within the series of written questions with which this dynamic little Scotsman had presented him. Knox had wanted to know whether the son of a king who inherited the throne as a minor ought to be obeyed; whether a woman ruler could transfer her rights to her husband; whether it was obligatory to obey laws which enforced idolatry; and whether nobility who opposed a monarch could be supported in certain circumstances. These questions clearly arose from the tense and delicately-balanced situation in England, and for the most part conflicted with Calvin's own views. He had always held that true and lawful monarchs ought to be obeyed. Although Calvin did not approve of women rulers he argued that they could hand over their rights to their husbands if it was in accordance with the law of the land. This answer was not what Knox wanted to hear. When Bullinger took a very similar line, Knox perhaps concluded that Switzerland did not offer him the opportunity he was seeking. He returned to Dieppe in April 'to learn the estate of England and Scotland', as he told Mrs Bowes in a letter, indicating that his sights were still fixed on a role within a British Protestant movement.

It has been suggested that Knox may have visited Germany on the way. This cannot be known for certain – he does not specifically refer to a German visit – but can be deduced from the publication of subsequent tracts in Emden. This is not in itself conclusive proof of anything, since the European

Protestants used various fictitious devices for their literature, some of which was satirically labelled as published in the Castel San Angelo, Rome, the pope's own home.

Back in Dieppe, his pen sharpened, in May *An Epistle to the afflicted brethren in England* was followed three weeks later by *A comfortable epistle sent to the afflicted Church of Christ, exhorting them to bear his cross with patience*. In the first, Knox says that the idolators will receive their deserts in this world as well as the next, but it is mild in tone. He alludes to his Swiss tour but says he cannot at this point commit to writing the subjects he discussed with the Swiss divines and adds that if he thought he could be in England without endangering others, he would be there. It is a comparatively restrained document. The second goes a little further and raises the question of vengeance for the injustices heaped on the Protestants in England. Knox makes a distinction between private and public vengeance which he was consistently to preserve in his thinking. The innocent guard cannot be killed during an escape but the system or ruler can be removed by force. Knox has taken the argument of the 'just war', which was used by the medieval theologians to underwrite wars *between* nation states, and applied it *within* the state. The idea that sovereignty could lie with the people within the state, rather than in an aristocracy, was a new and revolutionary doctrine, which is Knox's unique contribution to the Reformation and to political thought.

It is as if he was holding back in these two tracts, testing the waters, waiting for some news that would prevent him from drawing the devastating conclusion that for several years had been formulating in his mind. He was aware of it, as revealed in his questions to Calvin, but he was looking for confirmation. Now, as the summer came to Dieppe and Knox sat looking across the Channel to England, frustration was building up inside him, angrily feeding on the news of defections and appeasement even within his own former congregation. In this mood he sat down to write *The Faithful Admonition unto the professors of God's truth in England*.

This was his longest and most significant tract to date and in it the rhetoric took on a sharper and deadlier tone. It called for blood. He pungently attacked the Catholic bishops past and present: the 'Devil's Gardiner' and his 'blind buzzards', the 'wily Winchester', 'Bloody and butcherly' Bonner, 'dreaming Durham' (Tunstall); Knox declared that they deserved only death. There was special bitterness for the hypocrisy of William Paulet, the Treasurer, whom Knox again cast as Shebna, reminding his readers that it was Paulet who had cried that Mary was an incestuous bastard who would never reign in England, and who was now crouching and kneeling to her as a minister in her government. But the most controversial part of the Admonition is what Knox said about Mary herself, which shocked his Protestant readers almost as much as his Catholic ones.

Knox concludes that had Mary been put to death herself before she had had a chance to succeed to the throne the fruits of her cruelty could have been avoided. He cites evil women in the Bible who pale beside Mary's example:

Of Lady Mary who hath not heard that she was sober, merciful and loved the commonwealth of England? Had she, I say, and such as are now of her pestilent counsel, been sent to Hell before these days, then should their iniquity and cruelty so manifestly have appeared to the world . . . Jezebel, that cursed idolatress, caused the blood of the prophets to be shed, and Naboth to be murdered unjustly for his own vineyard; but yet I think she never erected half so many gallows in all Israel as mischievous Mary hath done within London alone. But you papists will excuse your Mary the Virgin-well, let her be your virgin and a goddess meet to maintain such idolaters.

He ends with a chilling prayer: 'Delay not Thy vengeance, O Lord, but let death devour them in haste; let the earth swallow them up and let them go quick to the hells. For there is no hope of their amendment, the fear and reverence of thy holy name is quite banished from their hearts.'

Even allowing for the hyperbole and rhetoric of the time, this outburst against Mary was excessive and does not show Knox in a good light. It was the product of bad temper, depression and frustration. She who was now Queen of England had deprived him of his vocation as a preacher, and had parted him from his fiancée and his closest friend (the Bowes women). Now the Queen by her marriage was about to undo the Reformation in England and probably open the way for the establishment of a Spanish-style Inquisition, which would see to it that any of Knox's former friends and supporters would deny their faith or die for it.

For Knox, this tract represents a crossing of the Rubicon. He realised that he had been defeated, that he could advance across the Channel but death would await him. In exile, retreat was meaningless and so he lashed out. But while we may dismiss the tract as a stream of bad-tempered bile, from that moment the ideas within it remain his thinking. He never repudiated the doctrines contained in the Admonition, which justly allow him to be called a revolutionary as well as a Reformer. The Admonition was a gut reaction to his circumstances at the time, but Knox had shown in submitting his questions to Calvin that he wanted to be able to justify his stance intellectually. In the beginning of the tract he admits 'how small was my learning and how weak I was of judgment when God called me to be his steward'. Thus, at that moment, with no revolution to lead, no congregation to minister to, Knox made virtue of necessity and journeyed once more to Switzerland in pursuit of the learning that he lacked.

He arrived in Geneva in the autumn of 1554 and began to study Hebrew for the first time, but a winter of bitter experience awaited him, not entirely of his making or choosing. The Marian persecutions had the effect of precipitating a second wave of emigrations from England. This time it was native-born Englishmen and women who fled to the European centres of protestantism in search of sanctuary. Frankfurt was one such centre. Linked by water along the Rhine and Main to Basle and the Scheldt, it was already the publishing capital of Europe and a free city of the Holy Roman Empire. Although sympathetic to Lutheranism, it had reached a truce with the Emperor and had won the right to harbour Protestant congregations. One such had been set up by the French Protestant Valerand Poullain and his Flemish weaver refugees who had transplanted there from Glastonbury. Now they were joined by a group of some two hundred English refugees led by William Whittingham, a radical Protestant. The French congregation had been granted permission by the Frankfurt authorities through Johann von Glauburg to hold services in the church of the White Ladies, and the English joined them. Being outside the system of patronage they were free to elect their own ministers and also to adopt the liturgical service they preferred. Whittingham lost no time in dispensing with the features of the Cranmer Prayer Book which he thought reminiscent of Catholic theology, and opted for Poullain's service, which contained Swiss elements.

Here in microcosm were the two wings of the English Protestant Church, those who believed that services should be regulated through a liturgy and those who favoured a looser framework. The initiative in Frankfurt had been taken by the radical group, something they had not enjoyed in Cranmer's Church of England. However other leaders of the Anglicans in exile were not so happy to see the 1552 Prayer Book abandoned so quickly. Cranmer, Ridley and Latimer were about to go to the flames in England as martyrs for the faith because of that book. How would it look if the stance taken by the martyrs was undermined by the implicit criticism of a group in Frankfurt? There was also the fact that many of the exiles hoped that one day they would return to England, and they wanted to keep the common currency of their faith, as represented and contained in the Prayer Book.

Thus, when the English Protestants in Frankfurt wrote inviting preachers to apply to become their minister, the shrewder ones were reluctant to minister to a divided congregation. Three of the notorious Lenten preachers of March-April 1553 were approached – Haddon, Lever and Knox. Frankfurt also invited the more scattered radical groups to join them; but Haddon wrote from Strasbourg saying that they did not want to leave Alsace; Grindal wrote independently to ask a former bishop called Scory to go from Emden to be their pastor; and the English congregation at Zurich, which included Lever, had also written to decline.

Frankfurt then pressured Knox, who did not want to leave Geneva. He asked Calvin's opinion and was told he should accept. On hearing this, Frankfurt promptly elected him and declined Scory's services. Knox arrived in November 1554 to find that Whittingham's order of service was much to his taste; but there was a minority who still wanted to retain the English Prayer Book. He had not been there a fortnight when a group from Strasbourg descended, led by Grindal, and tried to nudge them into adopting the Cranmer liturgy. A compromise was struck and Knox tried his best to work with it, but in December Lever also reached Frankfurt and proposed that they should use the new service at least until Easter, when they should vote again on it. Appointed as associate minister, Lever proved to be a Trojan horse, for in March there arrived in Frankfurt a powerful group of English refugees led by Richard Cox, Chancellor of Oxford University. Cox had been one of the principal architects of Cranmer's Prayer Book and had prospered in the brutish days of Henry VIII, when he had furthered his career by bullying churchmen into accepting Henry's divorce from Catherine of Aragon as legitimate. His penchant for burning any books which he considered unsound had earned him the nickname of 'Cancellor' Cox. He had not forgotten Knox's role in imposing the Black Rubric in the Prayer Book and saw his chance to get even. The way he did so was by a mixture of harassment, bullying and blackmail.

The group began by disrupting a Sunday morning service, repeating the responses of the Cranmer Prayer Book despite the fact it was not being used. Lever, who was conducting the service, did not seem to mind, but Knox, sensing dirty work afoot, responded in his afternoon sermon by attacking the oppressiveness of a Prayer Book which could result in Bishop Hooper being imprisoned for not wearing particular vestments. He went on to say that the Edwardian Anglican Church was still rife with the abuses of Henry VIII's era, such as holding more than one benefice (a direct hit at Cox who had held several under both kings). Angry exchanges took place outside the church. Lever showed his true colours by suggesting that Cox and his incomers had a right to membership. Knox knew that he was probably handing a majority to the pro-Prayer Book lobby by acceding to this demand, but in a gesture undertaken for the sake of preserving unity in the Church of England in exile, he concurred. Cox responded by immediately tabling a motion for the expulsion of Knox as minister, which, with the support of Lever's group, was carried in the vote. Cox and Lever then told Knox he was forbidden to preach.

Whittingham hot-footed to inform Glauburg, who was appalled at the prospect of the church of the White Ladies becoming the church where the dirty linen of English protestantism was washed in public. He told Poullain to attempt a solution. The latter convened arbitration talks at his house but these eventually broke up, with Cox stalking out when Knox objected to beginning the matins service with the words 'Lord open thou our lips', since they were of papist origin. During these sessions Knox received a private visit from one of Cox's party, Edward Isaac, who promised him favour would be shown if he backed down. When Knox declined, Isaac then hinted that if he did not comply he would find himself in serious danger. Knox threw him out with a ringing denunciation.

Knox and Whittingham then began to fight back. They petitioned the Frankfurt Council, which controlled religious practice, to invite the Swiss reformers to draft a service for the city. They also took the opportunity to poison the ears of the council against Cox and his company by linking them with the faction that had persecuted Hooper, recently executed by Queen Mary. Bishop Hooper was a sympathetic figure in Frankfurt because his German wife was living in the city. The council told the English congregation that they had had enough and that they were to use Poullain's service and be done with it. To everyone's surprise Cox leapt to his feet and agreed at once. Even more surprisingly, he and his group sat without a response passing their lips as Poullain's service (which was in all respects similar to Whittingham's and Knox's) was performed. Then they played their trump card.

Isaac approached the council with a document which quoted John Knox in nine statements, which were allegedly treasonable and seditious about Queen Mary and her husband Philip of Spain; and also quoted his Amersham reference to the Emperor as worse than Nero. The last charge was the one that shocked the council. The Emperor would not hesitate to crush a city which harboured someone who compared him unfavourably with Nero. They convened a meeting of the council within hours and Knox was suspended, while Whittingham was ordered to prepare a Latin translation of the disputed words. Meanwhile Knox attended service in the English church as a member of the congregation. As soon as he entered, Cox's party walked out. The next day the council washed their hands of Knox and decided formally to expel him from Frankfurt. That night he 'preached' at a farewell gathering and the next day, March 26, less than a fortnight after Cox had come to Frankfurt, Knox was on his way back to Geneva. Cox waited only two days before persuading Glauburg that it was necessary to re-introduce the Prayer Book service and when Whittingham tried to protest, Cox appointed himself superintendent and abolished the office of elders. Dragooned out of Frankfurt, the radical party dispersed. Most followed Knox to Geneva.

There is an element of black farce about the Knox versus Cox saga but it is worth telling for two reasons. The first is that it is well documented from a number of sources and tells us more about Knox. Yes, he pugnaciously rose to the bait, but he also tried to reach practical compromises and showed a generosity of spirit in dealing with his adversaries which they did not reciprocate, and which he does not always show in the historical accounts in which he writes about himself. The second thing it reveals is the deep antagonism, even at this early stage, within the English Church between the 'Anglicans' and the radicals. When Queen Mary died and Protestant Elizabeth ascended the English throne in 1558, the Anglican party was to triumph, but we can see that the seeds of the later Puritan secession can be traced back to the failure of the radical Protestants to gain the leadership of their church during the exile period. It was to be the prelatical types like Cox, and the manipulators like Cecil who were to determine the style of English religion from then on. Such a church would have no place for the likes of Knox.

That is the third reason why the 'troubles at Frankfurt', as a anonymous author described them, are important. They must have brought it home to Knox that, if ever there was to be a return from exile, in England he would be a marked man. Whether or not it is true, he would be blamed for the Marian persecution as a direct result of his Admonition. The charge does not hold up, since it can easily be shown that the policy of persecution was well in place before Knox's tract and that no one acted on its advice to rise against Mary. But (whether or not it is true) Isaac's charge against Knox was not the last time that the accusation would be made and it would make a return to England impossible for him in the future. Probably he did not consciously realise it at the time, but the year 1554 saw the end of his prospects in England. His actions throughout the next few years suggest that he did not admit this to himself until much later, but with the benefit of hindsight we can see that when the church door slammed behind Knox in Frankfurt, another door closed to him far away in England.

10

The Trumpet Sounds

When Knox returned to Geneva in April 1555 the city was not yet under the sway of Calvin. The Reformer had been driven from the city in 1538 and had returned in 1541. During the next fourteen years power alternated in a democratic see-saw between Calvin's party and an opposition group known as the Libertines, who opposed the stricter moral laws enforced by Calvin's Consistory. They were also resentful of the influx of pious Protestants to their city. Their leader was the Captain-General Ami Perrin.

Calvin's system of 'theocracy' was novel in several ways. Not only did the church have powers to bring moral offenders to task in addition to the powers of the magistrates, but the Calvinists applied their laws with an even-handedness that was no respecter of persons. It was against the law in most countries at the time to commit adultery, a law seldom enforced against the nobility. It was enforced in Geneva. While this zealous pursuit of vice could easily fall into pharisaism, in Geneva 'crimes' existed which broke new ground in human rights – such as punishment for spouse abuse or child neglect. It is easy to caricature the Calvinist obsession with provocative clothes or laugh at the censure on all-night dancing, but the oppression was not all on one side. When Madame Perrin was imprisoned for holding an all-night party she responded by trying to ride down a cleric in the street, on her horse. However her husband overstepped himself when in May 1555 he encouraged rioters to attack Calvin's house, where the Reformer was entertaining guests. Calvin seized his chance and Perrin was expelled with many of his followers, and from then on the Calvinists were supreme in Geneva.

Calvin was appalled at the way Knox had been treated in Frankfurt and gave him a warm welcome. Knox was now seeing Geneva at its best. The feuds and heresy hunts were all done with, and, applied with mercy, the theocratic discipline actually produced results. It could not have been a moral tyranny which attracted more than 6,000 refugees to the city during this period, swelling its population to 20,000. Knox must have found it an oasis after the banditry of the Castilian era, the tough life of the galley, the double-dealing of the English nobility and the duplicity of the Anglican exiles in Frankfurt. He called it 'the most perfect school of Christ that was on the earth since the days of the Apostles'.

Significantly, however, he did not stay long. He had been there four months when he received an invitation to return to Scotland. Mary of Guise's *laissez-faire* policy towards the Protestants, in order to gain their support for her power ploys, had changed the climate. Yet it is doubtful whether Knox would have made this journey across half of Europe on so flimsy a pretext as a change in the wind, without some real incentive. He had not been speaking Scots for six years. He had passed up the chance to go to Scotland previously. He now had in Geneva a ready-made congregation of devoted followers who wanted his ministry, without any Prayer Book to tangle the lines of communication. So why did he go? The answer is overwhelming in its persuasiveness. He went because at last he could be united with the two women who meant most to him. He went to get married.

Protestant refugees from England did not normally flee north from the Marian persecutions: they crossed the sea to Germany. But Elizabeth Bowes and her daughter were different. They had a web of contacts around Berwick and could easily slip into Scotland. The pressure on them to attend mass would have been growing. Probably the privileges of the Bowes family had protected them so far, but one cannot imagine that Sir Richard Bowes was happy about the danger in which his wife's religion was putting the family. If he gave his blessing to the flight from

Norham, it must have been a very mixed blessing. Was it relief to get rid of a wife who had caused him trouble by her obsession with this Scottish preacher? Was it concern for her safety and tinged with regret? I cannot believe that Bowes was happy about the way in which the terrible tensions which must have existed in his household were eventually resolved. A pointer to that is that neither Marjory nor Elizabeth returned until after his death, and, as we have seen, they had been cut out of his will. We can only guess at the feelings of the Bowes family when they learned that Marjory had chosen to elope with Knox, accompanied by her mother. Was it relief that they would not now attract persecution as Protestants, balanced by the likelihood that they would be the target of scandalous gossip? Or was it sadness to lose Marjory and Elizabeth, tarnished by bitterness at their decision to leave?

The marriage ceremony must have taken place in Edinburgh after Knox's arrival there in the autumn of 1555. There are no details of the event, but the honeymoon was a short one, as Knox had work to do. He went north with Erskine to Dun Castle near Montrose, leaving his wife and mother-in-law in Edinburgh, where the Protestant cause was not getting across as successfully as he had hoped. Back in Midlothian for Christmas, he stayed with Sir James Sandilands and there had a profitable meeting with three of the most powerful supporters of the Protestant cause: Lord Erskine (later Earl of Mar), Lord Lorne (later Earl of Argyll) and, most important, Lord James Stewart (later Earl of Moray), who had qualities of character which commanded trust from a wide variety of people, including Mary of Guise. He also met a young nobleman who was one of the rising stars at court, Sir William Maitland of Lethington, who had become a Protestant by intellectual conviction. Lethington clashed temperamentally with Knox and the two men were to become enemies in later years. He became known as the Scottish Machiavelli (or Michael Wily) and was said to be able to whistle and cluck with his mouth full [Mackie]

Knox's biggest success was in south-west Scotland. He wrote (to Mrs Bowes), 'The trumpet blew the old sound three days together', and lamented that if only he could have forty such days in Edinburgh he would die happy. An interesting footnote to the triumph in the west and south was that the court officials had heard that the preacher who was causing all the trouble was an Englishman. This could have been both because Knox had lost his Scots accent and because he preached in English, rather than the Scots tongue. But the emphasis on this visit was not on popular acclaim, rather on cultivating the leaders and lairds. In retrospect the Reformation in Scotland would not have happened had it not coincided with the wishes (and personal benefit) of the nobility and landowners. It had to be revolution from the top down. Knox celebrated communion as he went round the houses of the lairds, and set up stronger lines between the Genevan model of religion and Scots Protestant practices than his predecessors had ever been able to achieve. This also gained him a reputation as a contender for the leadership of Scottish protestantism, since at this time no such single figure existed.

Possibly fearful that one should emerge, the Archbishop of St Andrews, John Hamilton, and his bishops summoned Knox to appear at Black Friar's church in Edinburgh on May 15 1556 on a charge of heresy. Hamilton had been making some attempts at internal reform, the most notable being his catechism (now regarded as the work of John Winram). However he still retained his own concubine. Reform clearly did not begin at home. Nothing was done about the scandal of lay commendators holding the principal benefices in the Scottish Church. This meant that in the Scottish Parliament, composed of the Three Estates (nobility, church and burgesses), the church representatives (apart from the bishops) were not clerics at all. It was not so much that the counter-Reformation reached Scotland late as that it came too late to be of any use. The Catholic Church in Scotland in 1555 had passed the point where it was capable of reforming itself from within.

But it had still not lost its appetite for hunting heretics and Knox was high on the wanted list. The move to put Knox on trial backfired because he took up the challenge and appeared in Edinburgh together with a posse of Protestant lairds. With the possibility of violence arising, the bishops hastily backed down, with the approval of the Queen Mother, Mary of Guise, who was anxious lest her *laissez-faire* policy be undermined by making a martyr out of Knox. The Protestants used the postponement of the summons as the excuse for a rally of strength in Edinburgh. Encouraged by the turn-out and impressed by Knox's drawing power, they asked him to prepare a letter to Mary of Guise inviting her to become a Protestant.

In retrospect it was an absurd hope. Not only was the support of the Congregation patchy, but it was by no means loyal to the cause when circumstances changed, as Knox was to find out. Perhaps there was a diplomatic purpose behind the letter, to force Mary of Guise to give further concessions, but the sister of the man who was running the persecution of French Protestants was hardly likely to defect to the Protestant religion. She wrote to her brother the Cardinal of Lorraine a few months later, 'I am forced to keep up many pretences until I come to the proper time.' The proper time was the realisation of her consistently held policy of marrying her daughter Mary Queen of Scots in France in order to bring Scotland into France's domain. However the incident shows the leading position which Knox now commanded and the content of his letter shows how diplomatic and pragmatic he could be when he tried: 'I am not ignorant how dangerous a thing it appeareth to the natural man to innovate anything in matters of religion. And partly I consider that your Grace's power is not so free as a public reformation perchance would require . . .'

This was not the curser of queens and polemicist of the Admonition, but a cannier Knox. Nevertheless he hints that 'if the zeal of God's glory be fervent in your Grace's heart, by wicked laws ye will not maintain manifest idolatry'. The appeal fell flat. After reading the letter, which was formally presented by the Earl of Glencairn, Mary of Guise handed it to the Archbishop of Glasgow (James Beaton) with the dismissive words, 'Please you my lord, to read a pasquil [lampoon]'. When Knox heard in later years about the humiliating treatment his appeal had received, it inflamed him to bitter anger against the Queen Mother. Apart from its naïvety, the letter was a straw in the wind to which, astute politician that she was, Mary probably should have paid more attention. She does not show herself to have been aware of Knox as a significant figure, since she does not mention him in her voluminous correspondence, before or after this event. However her dismissal of the preacher as a nonentity made her an enemy who would not easily forget her.

Nor had Knox forgotten Geneva. The congregation there sent word that they had elected him minister in November 1555, and he was faced with a choice: to stay in his native land and complete the process he had started, or return to the haven in which he had found peace to study. He chose Geneva. In May 1556 he dispatched his family (which now included a servant, James, and a pupil called Patrick) to Dieppe and joined them in July. Why? Many biographers look for the explanation in later letters in which he says his reason for not rushing back to Scotland in 1557, was his fear that a calamitous civil war would result [letter to his sisters in Edinburgh, April 16 1558].

The belligerence of Knox's language and his key role in the revolution of 1560 have made it difficult to think of him as someone who wished to play down confrontation. Yet up to this moment he had been on the losing side of a number of conflicts and it is reasonable to assume that he would have wanted to be sure of victory before he embarked on a collision course with the Queen Regent and the Catholic establishment. He was convinced that the conditions for that victory did not as yet exist in 1556 and in retrospect it is easy to agree with him. His detractors have portrayed these tactical withdrawals as cowardice but it is fairer to say that he was not the kind of charismatic leader who courts martyrdom.

Another plausible and more personal explanation would be that Knox had seen precious little of the Bowes ladies since he had come to Scotland. By returning to Geneva he was opting for personal fulfilment and happiness, of which his life had had little so far. Knox's heart was in the cause; but should we be surprised that his heart was also moved by Marjory and that he was not yet ready for another political fight?

Before he left Scotland he drew up a kind of manifesto for Scots Protestants to follow, particularly in the matter of regular Bible reading. When he returned with his family to Geneva in September 1556 he was plunged into a new world. The adventurer-preacher now had new responsibilities. His letters to another lady who figured large in his affections, Mrs Anne

Locke of London, reveal his depressed state on return to Geneva, or, as he put it, 'now burdened with downbill cares'. He refers to:

> daily troubles in my domestic charge wherefore I have not been accustomed, and therefore are the more fearful, as in the administration of public things appertaining to the pure flock here assembled in God's name, do compel me often to forget, not only my most special friends but myself . . .

The busy pastoral life we can understand, but the domestic trouble? Is there behind this letter some tension with his mother-in-law? Perhaps the anticipated delights of Mrs Bowes's company were not so easy to enjoy in close day-to-day domestic confinement. In any case, was it disloyal of Knox to be writing to another woman friend? That he had other women correspondents in Edinburgh and London is documented, but Mrs Locke was special.

She was in her early twenties and the wife of a London merchant. Robert Louis Stevenson wrote, without any real evidence for his contention, that she was 'the only woman that Knox ever loved'. When the Marian persecution reached a height in the autumn of 1556 Knox wrote her another three letters imploring her and her friend Mrs Hickman to come to Geneva. In one he expresses the 'thirst and languor' which he has for her presence, and says 'Sometimes I sobbed, fearing what should become of you'.

Mrs Locke came to Geneva, leaving her husband behind, but tragically one of her children died soon after her arrival. The fact that at the same time Knox was writing to lady friends in Edinburgh, with no such imprecations to flee, could suggest application of a double standard and a hidden motive for inviting Mrs Locke to Geneva. But there is no evidence that her husband disapproved of the relationship and when she returned to London she lived with him until his death in 1571. There is no doubt that there was a 'meeting of minds' between Mrs Locke and Knox, for although they ceased to correspond after 1562, her two subsequent husbands (the first a fiery divine) showed distinctly Knoxian characteristics. But there is no evidence of an improper relationship with Mrs Locke, and Knox seems to have enjoyed a harmonious and happy home life with Marjory.

A further instance of Knox's close relationships with women outside his marriage is provided by a letter the following year to Janet Adamson, who was married to his friend the Clerk of Registrar, Sir James McGill. In response to her complaint that Sir James was cold towards her, Knox counselled her to stay with him and added a diplomatic touch in his letter: 'Your husband is dear to me, for that he is endowed with some good gifts, but he is more dear for that he is your husband.' Put bluntly, Knox much enjoyed the company and confidences of women, but was far from being a Don Juan.

Knox's attitude to women on a personal level was utterly different to the relationships he had with the three Queen Marys who altered his destiny in different ways. That observation was nowhere more obvious than in the next significant incident in Knox's life. Everything seems to have been quiet following his return to Geneva. Knox does not appear to have occupied much of Calvin's attention. Then in May 1557 a letter arrived from the lords of the Congregation (Lorne, Glencairn, Erskine of Dun and Lord James), saying that although the political situation was much as when he left in 1555, Mary of Guise was more tolerant towards the Protestants and they felt the time was ripe for a visit from him. Knox was not so sure, and he carefully consulted his congregation. He also asked the advice of Calvin, who said that he would be rebelling against God and 'unmerciful to his country' if he did not go to Scotland.

It was probably not the answer Knox wanted to hear. He had good reasons for not going at this time. Marjory had given birth in May to his first son, Nathaniel, and his friend from London, Mrs Locke, was distraught at the loss of her child. Furthermore France had begun to crack down on heresy (which included protestantism) and travel would not be so easy. Finally, under pressure from Spain, England declared war on France on June 7, and Knox's proposed journey from Dieppe to Scotland became dangerous in the extreme. Knox managed to delay reaching Dieppe until October 24. The news he received there from Scotland understandably caused his hot temper to boil over.

The lords had changed their minds. They advised him that the time for his return was not yet ripe. Knox immediately fired off a letter (October 27) in which he pointed out that it was not a small matter to leave his congregation in Geneva. He might have pointed out further that he had travelled 1,000 kilometres across a country in which he was liable to be arrested for heresy, only then to be informed that his services were no longer required. Typically Knox could not resist telling these aristocrats what he thought of them:

> Ye receive of your brethren honour, tribute and homage at God's commandment; not by reason of your birth and progeny (as the most part of men falsely do suppose) but by reason of your office and duty which is to vindicate and deliver your subjects and brethren from all violence and oppression, to the uttermost of your power . . . the reformation of religion and of public enormities doth appertain to more than to the clergy, or chief rulers called kings.

In our age the idea of social privilege being passed down through birth is universally called into question and Knox's opinions may not seem so radical as they were in the sixteenth century. His position went further than a reminder of the moral obligations of the nobility. Simmering beneath the surface of Knox's statement is a more egalitarian concept which goes beyond the anti-aristocracy position of his Admonition (and would soon go even further). Knox finished by roundly criticising the nobles for their inaction. He pointed out that Scotland had been enslaved and yet the lords supposed they were patriotic in supporting the war against England when a Protestant country ought to be neutral in a war between Catholic states. There was no reply from the lords, who must have been taken aback at the strength of the rebuke.

Knox stayed in Dieppe for two months waiting for news. Finally on December 17, his patience exhausted, he picked up his pen. This letter was gloriously inconsistent with the content of his first, and counselled the lords that they should do nothing which would subvert lawful authority and warned them that it would be sinful if they used the excuse of furthering religious ends to rebel against the sovereign for reasons of personal gain or secular motive. Knox's apologists say that he had begun to see what the Scottish lords were up to (especially Chatelherault, who was staging a comeback by aligning himself with the Protestant Congregation in a bid to advance the Hamilton dynasty). Knox's critics say that he was piqued and jealous that the Reformation in Scotland looked like going ahead without him as leader. There is a third explanation, namely that Knox's behaviour was showing signs of psychological stress. He was approaching another crisis in his life and the violent swings of his opinions are evidence of an internal debate in his mind about the question of revolution in Scotland. The two letters thus represent the two sides of the debate. Perhaps there are elements of truth in all three explanations.

Despite the temperamental way in which Knox developed his policies, and the inconsistency of his letters, his position moved consistently towards revolutionary ideas. Anger was the catalyst which brought out his energies and focused them towards a goal. Although it was not published until the spring of 1558, it was probably in Dieppe that he wrote his most famous tract, also directed against Mary Tudor and entitled *The First Blast of the Trumpet against the Monstrous Regiment of Women*. The title has sometimes been interpreted as an anti-feminine outburst, but Knox was anything but a misogynist. By 'monstrous regiment' Knox means unnatural rule, underlined by the fact that Scotland and England were both ruled by women at this time. While the medieval church's attitude to women was to revere them as chaste symbols and subjugate them as vassals, no such thinking is found in Knox.

We have seen that he was not a woman-hater; but it was this tract above all which earned him that reputation. He knew it would arouse controversy – he admits as much – and it was originally published anonymously. Most of it was concerned with a personal attack on Mary Tudor for her cruel persecution of Protestants. There are a few revealing touches: Knox writes as a British citizen, showing his aspirations were not yet moved from England to Scotland. He also dismisses the example of Deborah as a biblical example of female rule (not only did Bullinger justify female monarchs by reference to Deborah, but

Knox at a future date was happy to use her as an example when attempting to undo the effects of this tract after Queen Elizabeth came to the throne). His main point was that since a woman could not be a barrister or a judge, it was therefore an absurdity for a woman ruler to be head of the whole legal system and the source from which the judges derived their authority. In arguments like this Knox was striking at the root of the monarchy. He finished by going even further and preaching sedition:

> First [the estates and people] ought to remove from honour and authority that monster in nature; so call I a woman clad in the habit of a man, yea a woman against nature reigning above a man. Secondarily, if any presume to defend that impiety, they ought not to fear first to pronounce, and then after to execute against them the sentence of death.

Knox took the long way round on his journey back to Geneva but the time spent in transit did not dim his fiery mood. He travelled south to La Rochelle, the port from which Scotland's supplies of claret were shipped and where there was now a thriving Scots Protestant congregation. He performed a baptism there and, according to legend, made the prediction that he would be preaching in St Giles, Edinburgh within a few years. He arrived in Geneva to find he had been re-elected, along with Christopher Goodman, his Frankfurt ally, as joint-minister of the English-speaking congregation in December 1557.

For the next year Knox was prolific in writing polemics. Although Geneva was patrolled zealously for moral misdemeanours, there appears to have been free theological discussion and no high-handed control exerted over scholarly publications and tracts, such as Knox was issuing. In one of these Knox took up the insult that Mary of Guise had paid him (in dismissing the 'pasquil') and he redoubled his criticism of her. He then attacked the Scots nobles who had let him down. His *Appellation from the sentence pronounced by the bishops and clergy to the Nobility and Estates of Scotland* was nominally a defence of his denunciation for heresy after he had left Scotland, but in reality it was an attack on the nobility. It went even further

than the First Blast, and in it Knox confessed to have been the
author of the previous pamphlet.

Knox had now completely abandoned any support for
Tyndale, Luther and Calvin in their advocacy of Christian
obedience to rulers. He used Old Testament examples to argue
that God punishes people who do not rise up against the
ungodly. Standing their doctrine on its head he now argued that
it was the Christian duty of nobles to put idolaters to death.
Although God has ordered society into kings, nobility and
commonality:

> in the hope of the life to come He hath made them all equal
> . . . so constantly I affirm to you that it doth no less appertain
> than to your kings or princes to provide that Jesus be truly
> preached amongst you, seeing that without His true
> knowledge can neither of you both attain to salvation. And
> this is the point wherein I say, all man is equal.

This is the stuff of which revolutions were made in future
centuries and which must mark Knox out as one of Europe's
revolutionaries in intention as well as in deed. He went on to
exhort the common people to refuse to pay their tithes, since
by paying they were underwriting tyranny: if they paid tithes
to a corrupt church, they would be no better than the citizens
of Sodom or the soldiers of Pharaoh who paid the price of
complicity.

Knox and the Calvinists have sometimes been accused of
holding to a crude idea of predestination in which God has
arbitrarily divided humanity into the sheep and goats of the elect
and the damned. But Knox's view of the process of election
is here revealed as corresponding more to doing one's moral
duty as a necessary condition for staying within the ranks of
the elect. (During the next year Knox did write a rather turgid
defence of Calvin's doctrine of the elect, but it had little of the
hallmarks of his style and was probably written to appease Calvin
after the storm of controversy broke in Europe over the First
Blast.) One other significant work emanated from Knox's pen
at this time: *An admonition to England and Scotland to call them
to repentance.* In this Knox revealed that he intended that the

subject of the 'Second Blast of the Trumpet' (which was never published) would be that kings ruled not by birthright or blood-line but only by fulfilling their Christian duty, and that no people could be bound to obey tyrants who ignored these duties. This was even more radical than the First Blast.

However it was the First Blast which attracted howls of rage from all sides. The English Protestants in Strasbourg complained about it to Calvin, who was appalled. He was particularly embarrassed to discover that it had been printed in Geneva and would thus reflect on his own standing throughout Europe. This fear was justified, because when Mary Tudor died in November 1558 Elizabeth and her adviser Cecil took grave exception to it and wrote to Calvin, who quickly dissociated himself from the work. It has been suggested that Knox would never have written it had he been more aware of the mood in England at the time. The growing expectation was that Mary did not have long to live, and this encouraged Protestants to conform and bide their time. Knox's fundamental ideological objection to the mass as idolatry and to appeasement had isolated him as an extremist. Elizabeth never forgave him not only for the remarks about women, which obviously could be applied to her (despite Knox's attempt to make her an exception), but also because of his advocacy of armed revolt against monarchy.

Was it therefore a grave blunder to write the First Blast? In one sense it certainly was, because in hindsight it denied Knox the chance to re-enter England (his requests for visas were time and again laid aside by Cecil during the next few years). That denied him the opportunity to play a part in the English Reformation. It also put difficulties in the way of the creation of a British Protestant church and put paid to any chance that the radicals would be accepted back into the Anglican establishment in Elizabethan England. It is debatable whether the radical Protestants would ever have been able to play a significant role within the Church of England without placing strains on its unity. Their form of protestantism was basically incompatible with the type of Anglican establishment which eventually emerged. But whether or not he damaged his own standing and that of the radical Protestants in England, Knox's arguments were instrumental in bringing about the Reformation in Scotland. Certainly the Reformation could not have been achieved without the backing of the nobility, but neither could it have come about without an armed rebellion. Knox provided the justification for the latter.

Events in Scotland during 1557-8 were coming to a head. Mary of Guise had managed to displace Arran as Regent and now seized her chance to implement her plan to marry her daughter Mary Queen of Scots to Francis, heir to the French throne. The Protestant lords backed the proposed marriage in December 1557. Lord James Stewart and Erskine of Dun were members of the delegation which negotiated the terms in Paris. These contained a secret clause which allowed the Scots to control the succession to the Scottish throne if Mary should prove to be childless. The marriage was a source of even greater satisfaction to the French, for if Mary could hand Scotland over to them, they would control north Britain once and for all.

The Catholic bishops in Scotland tried to use the closer link with France to crack down on protestantism but this backfired badly. In April 1558 the octogenarian priest Walter Miln was burnt by Archbishop Hamilton in St Andrews. When the crowd saw the old man writhing in the fire, bound by a rope which had to be borrowed for the occasion, they broke through the cordon and cut him free so that he could have a merciful death. A cairn was erected on the spot and as soon as the authorities had it dismantled, it appeared again. The sense of outrage in the St Andrews area must have been reminiscent of the days of Wishart. But this time support for revolt was far more widespread than the Castilians had received. A riot on St Giles's Day (September 1) in Edinburgh resulted in a statue of the saint being smashed. In Tayside when a leading Protestant called Methven was outlawed, the burgesses refused to carry out the sentence.

When the news came to Scotland of Mary Tudor's death on November 17 1558, it buoyed the hopes of the Congregation that they could again count on English help. Among the congregations of English exiles in Europe the news was received with relief and many made their preparations to hurry back to England. But Knox received another piece of news at the same time. Through Geneva came a Scottish emissary named John

Gray on his way to Rome to ask for papal approval of the appointment of the new Bishop of Ross. With a canny eye for economy the lords of the Congregation had asked him to deliver a letter to Knox telling him that the time was now ripe and that he should come over and join them. They put in a note to Calvin asking him to twist Knox's arm to leave Geneva. It is not hard to imagine that Calvin would willingly have done so, since Knox's latest writings had shown such dangerous traits and had already embarrassed him.

It was almost a replay of 1557: Marjory had just given birth to their second son (Eleazar); and Knox had just been re-elected minister of the English-speaking congregation. Knox again procrastinated. Had he not seen all this before, and then been rebuffed at the eleventh hour? But the exodus of his congregation back to England, and probably a little pressure from Calvin, helped him to make up his mind. On January 28 1559 he left his family in Geneva and made for Dieppe, where he found the town in turmoil. A Protestant revival had been sweeping France and in May a crowd 10,000 strong had marched down the Rue St Jacques in Paris singing Protestant songs. Many prominent citizens had become Protestants and the movement was strong in Normandy, where Delaporte, the minister at Rouen, had been holding secret meetings in private houses. When an outbreak of plague prompted Delaporte's departure, Knox stepped into the breach. During his period as guest preacher several large public meetings were held where the Knox trumpet sounded the old sweet song. Despite the dangers the situation held, he clearly relished the role. In addition this delay served to put off the moment of decision. Would he return to England or to Scotland?

Significantly it was to England that he wrote first, asking for safe conduct through the country. He addressed his letter to the English Secretary of State, Sir William Cecil, whom he had known in his days as a court preacher. He soon got his reply. There was to be no way through. Soured and angry, on April 6 Knox was writing to Mrs Anne Locke in reply to her query about the suitability of the 1552 Prayer Book in the new situation, and he now went as far as to suggest that the book he had once used himself was sinful since it was man-made. He went on to reveal how raw his feelings had become:

for to me it is written that my First Blast hath blown from me all my friends in England . . . the Second Blast, I fear, shall sound somewhat more sharp, except men be more moderate than I hear they are . . . England hath refused me; but because before it did refuse Jesus Christ the less do I regard the loss of that familiarity.

Knox is here privately acknowledging that England is now a closed country to him. He did write again throughout April to Cecil – three times, in fact – but a study of these letters suggests that their request for safe passage cannot be taken at face value. They are to be interpreted as posturing by someone who has lost the game. Knox indulges in cutting irony about Cecil himself, for his appeasement, 'although worthy of hell, (God) hath promoted you to honours and dignity'. He breaches etiquette, addressing the Queen's Majesty as 'Queen Elizabeth' (when he knew better). He concludes one cheeky letter with an offer: that he will admit Deborah as an exception to the rule about women rulers, if the Queen will admit that he is correct in general! This is hardly the stuff of which successful petitions are made and one suspects that Knox is indulging himself and getting his irritation out of his system by prolonging the exchange. Cecil simply did not bother to reply. Knox was *persona non grata* in England and would remain so. Thus John Knox set sail in late April from Dieppe for Scotland. He had exhausted his options. There was now only one thing for him to do – to take up the two-handed sword once again.

11

Revolution and Reformation

Knox landed at Leith on May 2 1559. The news was quickly passed to the Catholic bishops, who were meeting two miles inland at Edinburgh, congratulating themselves that the Queen Regent, Mary of Guise, had summoned four of the leading Protestant preachers to appear before the Privy Council on charges of sedition. Here was a chance to net another one. They sent immediate word to Mary in Glasgow. Meanwhile Knox made for Dundee where a large show of strength had gathered round the preachers. This trick had worked before for the Congregation and the summonses had been withdrawn. On that occasion the Regent had not wished to risk civil war as it would have undermined her diplomacy, which depended on dealing with both factions. But this time she called their bluff and did not withdraw the summons. The stakes were raised, for if the Protestants marched in strength to Stirling to defend their preachers before the Privy Council, then they would be in open rebellion.

Within one week of his return Knox found Scotland on the brink of civil war and had himself been outlawed by proclamation in Glasgow. The reasons for this rise in the political temperature can be traced to the fear that, once the young Mary Queen of Scots was married to the Dauphin Francis, Scotland would be run as a province from France. The Protestants felt that some action was now inevitable.

By one of those tiny coincidences through which fate seems to have a hand in history, on the same ship which took Knox from Dieppe to Leith was a government messenger carrying the new seal of Scotland. It bore the arms of the three countries which most affected the preacher's fate – Scotland, England and France. Now that the heir to the French throne had been granted the crown matrimonial of Scotland, and the English throne was occupied by a sovereign who, in the eyes of the Roman Catholic Church, was technically illegitimate and therefore ineligible to hold it, Mary Stuart combined in her person the destinies of all three nations. She had been nurtured in France with two aims: first to bring Scotland under French rule; and second, through her claim as the great-granddaughter of Henry VII of England, to transfer the English crown to the Guise family.

There were several factors which affected the religious situation in Scotland in 1559: the battle for the throne; the rivalry among the Scottish nobility; the support for militant protestantism among the common people; and the Roman Catholic establishment. These four variables could have produced several outcomes. Mary of Guise, the Queen Regent, was working to secure for Scotland the old model of church and state in which the monarch espoused the Catholic Church. However she had somewhat compromised her position by relying for support on the section of the nobility which supported the Protestant religion. These nobles were in turn being encouraged by the English government to push for a Lutheran-style Reformation (on the Danish model), or else a system like their own in which the monarch dictated church policy. The Scottish nobles were not in any position to deliver such an outcome. To begin with, they were not a majority, and they only had the support of Mary of Guise on a limited basis. There was no possibility that she would take the initiative to form a new church independent of Rome. This had been the decisive factor in England and one which would be necessary in Scotland to achieve a Reformation on the English or Danish models. The Queen Regent had proved herself an able and astute leader in a foreign country which, to her, must have seemed bleak in contrast to the sophistication of the French court. The other group which might have brought about change, the militant Protestants, were not yet strong enough in numbers, except in certain areas, to do anything on their own, since the Catholic Church's officials dominated the system of law-enforcement. Apart from holding on to power, the Catholic Church did not have the resources to reform itself or to command popular allegiance.

It was an uneasy stalemate and a breakthrough could only be achieved when the militant Protestants were able to ally themselves with the nobility. This is what indeed happened and it brought about the Scottish Reformation. Ironically it was the Queen Regent herself who made it happen. Her skill in balancing the rival factions among the nobility, and her deft supplanting of Arran, showed considerable political acumen. However after she had achieved her first aim of uniting the Scottish and French crowns she became more confident and, with a substantial French army at her command, began to force the pace. When Erskine of Dun requested that she withdrew the summons for the preachers to appear at Stirling, she did not do so. By this time the preachers and their 'army' of supporters had advanced as far as Perth. This was within Protestant territory, but they hesitated to take the fateful step of marching west towards Stirling.

The Queen Regent, who was now suffering bad bouts of gout, was in no mood to back down. Although Knox had been busy sending out letters declaring that the Congregation was loyal to the young Queen and the Regent, and was only seeking a reformation of religion, the Privy Council was unimpressed and duly put the preachers to the horn (that is, outlawed them). Anyone who assisted them was declared a rebel. This news was brought to Perth the next day (May 11 1559) and Knox was invited to preach in the church of St John the Baptist, the largest and most centrally-situated church, which was then heavily adorned with religious relics. Knox preached trenchantly on his favourite theme of idolatry. After the service, while the congregation were still milling around, a riot broke out when a priest attempted to celebrate mass at a side altar and a boy threw a stone at him, which missed and struck the monstrance in which the Host was displayed. This was the cue for wholesale iconoclasm, which resulted in nearby friaries being looted.

Knox tried to dissociate himself from the excesses of the mob,

which he called 'a rascal multitude', but this comes over as
disingenuous. In preaching such an inflammatory sermon he
effectively let loose the dogs of civil war. That is not putting
it too strongly, for civil war is how the Regent regarded the
situation and she called on her commander, d'Oysel, to march
on Perth. D'Oysel's command was 1,500 French soldiers and
another 500 Scots mercenaries. The Regent then asked the
Scottish nobility to support her against the rebels and they all
did so, including the minority Protestant nobility. She put
Chatelherault in charge of this second company. Even lords of
the Congregation, such as Lord James Stewart, did not approve
of the Perth insurrection. They were happy to use the
Congregation as a lever against the Regent but recent events
in Perth smacked of the Muntzer revolt in 1525 when the
peasants, inflamed by revolutionary ideas, tried to rise against
the nobility. That rising was ruthlessly suppressed as a threat
to the existing order and Martin Luther was one of those who
agreed that the followers of the radical preacher Thomas
Muntzer should be put to the sword.

Why then did the Perth Protestants not suffer the same fate?
Originally their only leaders among the nobility were Erskine
of Dun and Lord Ruthven, the Provost of Perth, but when
within a few days of the riot the latter defected to join the
Regent, they were left with only Erskine and Knox. This
appeared to increase the similarity with the Muntzer rebellion,
since in Knox there was a fiery preacher who had made it clear
that he was prepared to topple the existing order, and who held
extreme views about monarchy. But Knox had a trump card
up his sleeve in the relationships he had cultivated among the
nobles and soon had the chance to play it.

Men were pouring into Perth from Angus and Fife. The
commanders of the Regent's army, d'Oysel and Chatelherault,
were reluctant to join battle despite the fact that the forces facing
them would have been much less experienced in battle. Instead
they agreed to let Lord James Stewart and the Earl of Argyll
seek a truce. Although these Protestant lords did not support
the insurrection they knew that if there was bloodshed in Perth
it would precipitate a bitter and bloody civil war. Knox had
credibility with both men and took the opportunity to reassure

them that this was not an uprising against the state. While these talks were taking place, the Earl of Glencairn was harvesting the seeds of protestantism planted by Knox during his preaching tour in Ayrshire in 1555. Glencairn was able to raise 2,500 supporters for the cause (half of them mounted), whom he marched towards Glasgow. There he received a warning that on pain of treason he should not proceed. He was blocked by a detachment of d'Oysel's troops at the river Forth, so he swung to the north of Stirling along the road to Perth. This manoeuvre would have brought him up neatly behind the Regent's forces.

The fact of a large army approaching his rear was enough to persuade d'Oysel to offer terms to the Perth Protestants. The latter willingly agreed to disband their army and return home. The French forces promised they would not enter Perth and that a pardon would be given to the rebels. No doubt they confidently expected to mop up the rebels one by one at a future date, a well-tried method that many regimes have employed when faced with a popular uprising. Lord James's and Argyll's roles in the negotiations provide the key to this agreement, because they made it clear that if the Regent broke her word they would switch sides.

Switch sides they did, for no sooner had the rebels dispersed than d'Oysel sent the Scots mercenaries into Perth (claiming they were technically not French troops). As they passed the house of a prominent Protestant merchant, muskets were fired and his adolescent son was killed. Although the Regent claimed the shooting was accidental, the bitter anger felt at the child's death proved to be a recruiting agent for the Congregation and they called on their supporters to meet in St Andrews on June 11.

The wheel had come full circle since the days of the Castilians, and St Andrews seemed about to witness a re-run of the events of 1547. However, there were several important differences between the Castilians' *putsch* and the situation in 1559. The Cardinal's killers were hot-bloods drawn from the young Fife lairds, who did not have support from the Protestant areas of Tayside, Lothian and Ayrshire. The present rebellion had succeeded in winning countrywide support. The political and religious climate was also much more disposed to desperate measures. The Catholic Church had done little to reform itself since 1547 and the Protestant movement now had a much more sympathetic following. There was little justification for associating it with an unpatriotic alliance with the English. Patriotism now demanded that something should be done to prevent Scotland becoming a province of France.

Perhaps it was this last factor that persuaded Lord James to take the side of the Congregation and muster with the Protestants. His role is the most complicated of all in these events. Even after this episode, he continued to command the affection of Mary of Guise and visited her on her death-bed. He stood high in the counsels of Mary Queen of Scots yet he never compromised his allegiance to the Protestant religion once he had joined. As an illegitimate son of James V he had no legal claim to the throne of Scotland but equally he appears never to have entertained ambitions in that direction. Here he was, Prior of St Andrews, preparing to enter the town with a 'rascal multitude' who would not hesitate to do what they had done to Perth and gut the very priory of which he was head.

Lord James remains one of the most interesting and contradictory characters of the Scottish Reformation and certainly one of the most respectable. His dealings with both sides never earned him the same reputation of deceit and self-serving as that of Maitland of Lethington. His loyalty was considered far above that of the turncoat Lord Ruthven, who rejoined the Congregation in July 1559 after deserting it a month earlier. The French commander, d'Oysel, wrote that he could never understand the Scots nobility, 'who could be with you at breakfast and have gone over to the other side by dinner'. Lord James has been described as combining the spiritual temperament of a Puritan with natural charm and diplomacy. An unlikely friend and ally of Knox, the two men had evident respect for one another. Knox conducted Lord James's marriage and gave his funeral eulogy. (However there was a two-year rift after Lord James became Earl of Moray, when an embittered Knox turned against most of the lords of the Congregation.)

Prior to the gathering in St Andrews, Knox went round the south-east corner of Fife, the 'East neuk', preaching and precipitating a wave of iconoclasm. The Protestant martyr

Walter Miln had been arrested in Dysart, at the west end of this crescent of tiny fishing villages with horseshoe harbours, and his memorial cairn in St Andrews, still keeping his memory alive a year after his death, was soon to be enlarged by the smashed relics from the cathedral. The Regent was staying at Falkland Palace in mid-Fife and at her behest Archbishop John Hamilton moved back to St Andrews, warning that Knox would be shot if he tried to preach in the cathedral town.

Ignoring the threat, a very different Knox from the trembling tutor of 1547 entered the pulpit of Holy Trinity church on June 10 1559. He took as his theme the cleansing of the temple, and the men of St Andrews needed no clearer invitation for iconoclastic activity to begin in earnest. The priory and monasteries of St Andrews were devastated. Knox wrote to Mrs Locke in London, who was then providing his point of contact with Geneva: 'I did occupy the public place in the midst of the doctors, who to this day are dumb, even as dumb as their idols who were burnt in their presence.' That remark clearly reveals Knox's lack of respect for the scholastic theorists. He was an artisan of ideas, valuing them for the use to which they could be put.

These were heady days, and when the Regent's forces marched towards St Andrews the Congregation had already anticipated them and marched to head them off at Cupar where a heavy mist descended. The men of Dundee had shipped cannon from Broughty Ferry Castle and reinforcements 'rained from the clouds'. Thus when the mist lifted d'Oysel was faced with 3,000 men armed with cannon. Outnumbered, he offered a pardon if the Congregation would disband and burn no more abbeys. The Congregation refused and instead offered d'Oysel a truce for six days, although they could not resist burning Lindores Abbey, a few miles away on the road to Perth. They arrived back at Perth on June 24 and the 400-strong garrison agreed to vacate the city if they were not relieved within twelve hours. Thus another bloodless victory was won.

Two miles north of Perth stands the historic abbey of Scone where the kings of Scotland were crowned, and whose prior, Patrick Hepburn, had played a leading role in the Miln martyrdom. Hepburn promised to vote in the Scots Parliament with the lords of the Congregation if they spared the abbey. The Taysiders were having none of it. They rushed to claim their prize and Knox hurried to mediate. Knox the pragmatist realised that men like Prior Hepburn would be needed to make the revolution stick. However he does not seem to have been too dismayed when, after an illegitimate son of the bishop ran his sword through a man from Dundee, the crowd held back no longer and burned Scone to the ground. Knox quotes with approval an old woman onlooker who declared that the place had always been a 'den of whoremongers' where 'wives have been adulterated and virgins deflowered by the filthy beasts which hath been fostered in this den'.

One suspects that Knox was in his true element among these blunt-natured Pictish Scots of the east coast. The people who compiled the *Good and Godly Ballads* should certainly not be thought of as dark-browed Puritans. They shared the same kind of earthy humour which more sophisticated readers find it difficult to sympathise with in Knox. The ballads which the congregation might have been singing from the Wedderburn brothers' book, prior to a Knox oration, were not all Genevan metrical psalms and decidedly not the schmaltzy stuff of revivalist rallies. They had secular versions to the same tunes with which the congregation would have been familiar, songs about 'parish priests, the brutal priests' and others about nuns who 'cast up their bums and heaved their hips'. The peasants and artisans of the Congregation were the lumpen proletariat of a revolution, not the beady-eyed commissars of a regime.

Stirling and Linlithgow were next to be sacked, and although many began to return home, the Congregation's force of 1,300 men marched into Edinburgh. They encountered little resistance, for the demoralised Regent had withdrawn her forces to the safety of the French garrison at Dunbar in East Lothian. Knox preached in St Giles's, on this occasion a less inflammatory sermon, in which he stressed that the Congregation were not rebels against the sovereign but simply required a reformation of religion. The speed of events – seven weeks since the Perth *putsch* – had been remarkable but Knox knew that the situation was still delicately poised. The Treaty of Cateau-Cambresis between France, Spain and England in April 1559 and the depleted funds of their respective treasuries had made neither France nor England particularly eager to get involved in Scotland. Knox knew that sooner or later the French would have to act and he had been peppering Cecil with letters, requesting support and stressing that the ultimate aim of the Protestants was to expel the French from Scotland.

The English reaction was guarded. Cecil was no admirer of Knox and although the latter's status had been raised to that of a national leader, he was not a person with whom Elizabeth would do business: 'For his learning, as the matters now be, has no small credit, nevertheless his name here is not plausible.' [Cecil to Percy, July 11]. Although they were not displeased to see the French hold over Scotland slipping, the English church leaders and nobility were appalled at the destruction of the monasteries, and in his replies to the Scots Cecil hinted that if someone like Chatelherault came over to their side, then perhaps the Protestants could be recognised by some kind of treaty. Cecil had already arranged for Chatelherault's son, who had succeeded to the title of Earl of Arran, to be brought back from France where he had joined the Protestant movement. But the English were stalling. Cecil had told Percy, the Warden of the Marches, his link with Scotland, that the Scots could be given promises, money and men in that order: and presently there was no money.

Cecil continued to ignore Knox's pleas for active assistance but was anxious not to break off links with Scots Protestants. He sent a message to Knox through Percy that he would meet him secretly in England on condition that he could bring guarantees from the lords of the Congregation. The double-dealing correspondence between the English government officials and their Scots 'allies' has been picked over time and again. Knox, with his blunt confrontational style, was not a sufficiently adept player for the game of diplomacy but he insisted on taking part. On June 28 he had written to Cecil, 'We mean neither sedition nor yet rebellion against any just and lawful authority', and was arguing for 'a perpetual concord between these two realms'. At the same time he insisted on writing through Cecil to Queen Elizabeth, knowing that he was 'odious' to her, exhorting her to 'forget your birth and all title

which thereupon doth hang and consider deeply how, for fear
of your life, you did decline from God and bow to idolatry'.
Cecil probably chose not to pass the letter on. One fact which
emerges from the correspondence is that they both knew that
the French would retaliate at some point.

The death of Henry II of France from an eye wound in a
tournament on July 10 1559 proved to be the decisive event
which moved matters to a crisis. Francis II was now King of
France and Scotland, and dispatched reinforcements to the
Queen Regent. England was extremely wary of getting into a
war with France and still did nothing publicly to assist the
Congregation, to the intense frustration of Knox who fired off
more letters to Cecil. Privately Cecil advised Percy to do
everything 'in your endeavour to kindle the fire', but Protestant
morale was sinking. If the English would not help them now,
when would they? Meanwhile the Congregation continued to
proclaim its innocence of sedition in public, while assuring the
English in private that everything they were doing was directed
at getting rid of the French.

Suddenly on July 23, hoping to take advantage of the weakness
of the Congregation, the Queen Regent marched on Leith, where
the French fleet was expected, and set her forces in position,
looking up to the Congregation's depleted troops perched on
Calton Hill: the line of sight is now the broad street known as
Leith Walk. Less than a mile away the Governor of Edinburgh
Castle, Lord Erskine, commanded the streets of Edinburgh with
his cannon. Finding themselves caught between Erskine's
cannon and the deep blue sea of Leith, the lords of the
Congregation decided to make the best of the situation. They
agreed to a six-month truce which recognised the Regent's rule
except in matters of religion. In addition they gave up the Mint,
which they had seized, and promised to stop attacking church
property and withholding tithes. The preachers and Cecil
realised that the initiative they had gained had been thrown
away.

At this point Knox went on the secret mission to England
as emissary of the Congregation. He sailed from Pittenweem
in Fife round to Holy Isle in Northumberland, where there were
still many people who remembered him from his days in Berwick

and Newcastle. To the fury of the English, he was recognised. Negotiating with Knox was not something the English officials wanted to be seen doing. In his talks with Sir James Croft, who was close to the Queen and Cecil, Knox asked for troops and aid. Croft replied that neither could be promised until the Scots appointed someone in real authority. Knox suggested Lord James Stewart as the leader and indicated that Chatelherault had promised to come over to their side if French troops were not withdrawn from Scotland. He probably mentioned this latter possibility less than enthusiastically: Knox was always suspicious of the man who had led the army against the Castilians and whose motives were to advance the Hamilton dynasty. It must have been obvious to Knox that he was *persona non grata* with England's rulers, and he readily agreed to the suggestion that someone like Henry Balnaves should take his place in the negotiations when he returned to Scotland.

There he found that the lack of positive English support was making many of the brethren waver in their support for the cause. Knox fired off letters to Cecil, in one of them naïvely asking him to send troops which Elizabeth could publicly disown afterwards. Cecil crushingly replied that he could hardly do such a thing without it being transparently obvious what was happening. He did do Knox one favour, however, and that was to allow his family a safe passage through England. (Throckmorton, the English ambassador in France, who had arranged the secret return of young Arran, was able eventually to get the Knox family through, although their journey from Paris to Fife took all of three months.)

The stresses were beginning to tell on Knox. He had a recurrence of ill-health in August, probably brought on by the exhausting pace of his life. His spirits were raised on September 20 when his wife and family arrived. They were accompanied by Christopher Goodman, Knox's associate minister in Geneva, who had been a friend since the episode at Frankfurt and whose presence he had desired 'almost as much as that of my own dear flesh'. However the Congregation was no further forward. The Scottish harvest was in and although there was still no sign of English help or money, the lords of the Congregation felt confident enough to stage a march on

Edinburgh in mid-October. The Queen Regent retreated from the palace of Holyrood House into Leith and fortified the town. The lords of the Congregation were stymied. Worried that the French could easily get help to her through the port, they decided to make a gesture and formally deposed her as Regent in a ceremony in the Edinburgh Tolbooth on October 21 and proclaimed their loyalty to Queen Mary and King Francis in France. Chatelherault was declared Regent of Scotland for the second time in his life. It was a gesture that in the atmosphere of anarchy and stalemate meant little, except that the Hamiltons were back in the game on the side of the Congregation. That might explain why Knox was so lukewarm in his commendation of the move, stressing that the Congregation must have clear motives; and he even went on to argue that if Mary of Guise showed herself willing to submit to the nobility, she should be reappointed.

In the weeks that followed, the Congregation suffered a series of setbacks. Money (£3,000 wrung with great difficulty from England) eventually crossed the border on October 31, to be intercepted by the young Earl of Bothwell on behalf of the Queen Regent. There were skirmishes in which the Congregation came off worst and defections were biting deep into morale. Knox writes of that period: 'Many fled away secretly and those that did abide (a very few excepted) appeared destitute of counsel and manhood.' On November 6 the French attacked the food convoy coming into Edinburgh and the Congregation was forced to retreat out of the city, to the glee of the Catholic community. 'We would never have believed that our natural countrymen and women could have wished our destruction so unmercifully and have so rejoiced in our adversity.' Knox had tasted victory but it was bitter-sweet.

12

Ruler of the Roost

In many respects the four action-packed months which have so
far been charted represent the apex of Knox's career. He had
stepped off the ship at Leith at the beginning of May as a widely
known, and slightly notorious figure in Scotland. In those four
months his sermons had provided the match to light a bush fire
of religious revolt. Knox was not thereafter consigned to
obscurity, but from now on he does not lead the movement. The
initiative passed to the lords of the Congregation, and to the
English politicians. Knox had tried his hand at diplomacy and
failed miserably. It was not his game. It brought out the worst
in him, for his bluntness did not persuade his listeners and his
attempts to play politics make him seem untrue to his radical
ideals. Power games are not the preacher's best suit and Knox
was primarily a preacher. His relations with English protestantism
(in which he still thought he had a role to play) had repercussions
upon his policy of winning English support for the cause.

His letters to Cecil were ignored, or tolerated for the sake of
damage limitation: 'I like not Knox's audacity. His writings do
no good here and therefore I rather suppress them, and yet I mean
not but that ye should continue in sending of them' [Cecil to Croft
and Sadler, November 3 1559]. The real business after the
autumn of 1559 was done with the lords of the Congregation,
with whom Knox still had influence but who did not share his
vision of the future pattern of reformed religion in Scotland.
Policy was now in the hands of the Great Council of thirty
notables, dominated by the nobles but including eight lairds and

the Provosts of Edinburgh, St Andrews and Dundee. Knox was not even a member of the council set up to direct Congregation policy. This consisted of Chatelherault and his son Arran, Argyll, Lord James Stewart, Glencairn, Ruthven, and six lairds (Maxwell, Erskine of Dun, Pittarrow, Balnaves, Grange, and Halyburton, Provost of Dundee). Religious policy was directed by a group consisting of Knox, Willock and Goodman plus the newly-recruited Bishop of Galloway, Alexander Gordon.

Even if he was excluded from the political councils, there was a task for a man like Knox to perform at this time when the Lethingtons and the Chatelheraults were wheeling and dealing. His power as a polemicist was put to use in writing a history of the struggle, which would demonstrate that the Congregation was not out to usurp the monarchy. It is significant that publication of this account (Book II of the *History of the Reformation*) was suppressed by Knox during his lifetime. He took no pleasure in recalling the events of these days, perhaps also because he felt he had failed himself by getting his hands dirty in the battles of 1559.

Despite the way that he felt, November of that year was the occasion of one of his finest sermons and demonstrated that his true greatness was as a preacher. The Congregation had regrouped at Stirling Castle and Chatelherault was now sitting as the leading lord of the Congregation. Knox could not resist the irony of their former adversary becoming their leader. Preaching from Psalm 80 he said:

I am uncertain if my lord's Grace hath unfeignedly repented of that his assistance to those murderers unjustly pursuing us . . . but let it be so that he hath done (as I hear he has confessed his offence before the lords and brethren of the congregation); yet I am assured that neither he, neither yet his friends, did feel before this time the anguish and grief of heart which we felt when in their blind fury they pursued us.

Knox said what other people were undoubtedly thinking. He played down the talk of how Chatelherault's extra forces were to be their salvation. There was but one salvation, for 'I doubt not but that this cause (despite Satan) shall prevail in the realm of Scotland. For as it is the truth of the Eternal God, so shall it once prevail, howsoever for a time it may be impugned.' It was masterly stuff. He got in his gibe at his old enemy but succeeded in turning the occasion into a rallying call for a crusade. We have not only Knox's version of the incident, but other accounts testifying to the electric effect of this oration.

The Congregation dispersed, committed to regrouping in December. Knox went with Marjory to St Andrews, where she acted as scribe, not only for his *History* but for his regular letters to England and Geneva. He kept badgering Cecil, predicting that if French revenge was inflicted on Scotland, England would be next and so should do everything to help the Congregation, which was desperately short of funds. He even raised some himself through Mrs Locke, who helped organise a collection in London [Knox to Anne Locke, November 18].

During these five months Knox also sat as a member of the Kirk Session, which heard discipline cases. The records of these cases prove that prior to the Scottish Reformation there was a system in place for dealing with moral offences on the Geneva model. Most offenders were simply admonished if they repented, but some were outspoken in their criticism of Knox himself. This was all taking place in St Andrews, still the headquarters of the Catholic Church, although a considerable number of priests in the town had converted to protestantism. One of the bizarre footnotes to this period is that Knox, together with John Douglas, the Rector of the University, and Sub-Prior John Winram, his former adversary (both now converted), was trying the case of a woman whose husband accused her of adultery after two neighbours had peeped through cracks and seen his wife's lover remove his hose in her bedroom and then blow out the candle. The record shows that they found the woman not guilty!

Although Knox held the view in common with many of his era that adultery should be punished by death, in practice the Calvinist punishment for proven adultery was excommunication. In Protestant terms this did not necessarily spell eternal doom but rather being boycotted by the society in which they lived. The system was not yet as thorough as Geneva's, but it was working. Church attendance was compulsory for those who professed the faith and the distribution of admission tokens provided an effective way of checking attendance. Knox differed from Calvin in that he refused baptism to the children of unmarried mothers (on the grounds that the fact of baptism did not affect the destiny of their eternal soul, and that he regarded the Catholic doctrine of purgatory as superstition). Faced with refusal to baptise the child unless they provided the name of the father, many unmarried mothers were willing to 'shop' the father, since they believed the child would go to hell without baptism. This enabled the Kirk Session to summon him for his offence of fornication. When uncaringly administered, the system was tyrannical in the hands of the 'unco guid'; but there is no evidence that Knox was more severe than his brother ministers – indeed he is said to have been more lenient [Ridley, p. 371].

John Knox was not the only preacher in Scotland at this time although his was the voice of the Protestant church. The religious council was dominated by Knox and his protégé Christopher Goodman, who shared his views, but John Willock was equally influential in ecclesiastical matters. Willock, Knox's colleague in St Giles, has been credited with the authorship of much kirk doctrine and practice. He was born in Ayr, became a friar but emigrated to England in 1539, then, on Mary's accession, fled to Emden where he entered the service of the Countess of Emden who sent him as an emissary to Scotland in 1555. He was one of the group Knox met on his flying visit to Scotland that year to gather support among the nobility. Willock was less provocative than Knox in his preaching in St Giles during the 1559–60 period. But all the Protestant preachers were then in danger of assassination, particularly in Edinburgh because of its strong Catholic adherence.

In civil and religious wars the family feuds are always the most bitter. Among the leaders of the Protestant movement were some who would have been regarded by their families and former friends as defectors and traitors. One such was John Winram, whom we have already met in his role as Sub-Prior and St Andrews academic. His scholarly abilities qualified him to be chosen as interrogator at the heresy trials of Wishart, Adam Wallace and Walter Miln. Yet such were Winram's personal qualities that he was welcomed into the Reform movement and soon played a leading role. John Douglas, the Principal of the University of St Andrews, was probably brought into the

Reformed Church by the influence of Winram. He does not appear to have left written work or strong opinions but achieved notoriety in old age when he became one of the 'tulchan bishops' in 1571 (see p. 164). John Craig, a protégé of Knox's at St Giles and roughly the same age, embraced Lutheranism as a young monk and found his way to Italy, where he discovered Calvinism in a Jesuit library at Bologna. He escaped death at the hands of the Inquisition in Rome before returning to Scotland in 1560. Members of Craig's family remained active Catholics. John Row was born near Stirling and after studying law in Italy became a canon lawyer in the Vatican for the Archbishop of St Andrews. On return to Scotland as a Protestant convert he became the minister of the Congregation at Perth in 1560. John Spottiswood was educated at Glasgow and went to England where he became a friend of Cranmer's. Returning to Scotland, he settled in Lothian and was one of the first superintendents of the Reformed Church and the man who crowned James VI of Scotland in 1567. Of these men, Willock, Winram, Douglas, Row, Spottiswood and Knox were the six 'Johns' entrusted with drawing up the Confession and the First Book of Discipline, which was the blueprint of the new Scottish Church.

The creation of such a church was by no means inevitable or even probable as 1559 drew to a close. There was still no sign of English help and Knox was plunged into deep gloom. He wrote to Mrs Locke on the last day of the year:

> One day of troubles since my last arrival in Scotland hath more pierced my heart than all the torments of the galleys did the space of nineteen months; for that torment for the most part, did touch the body, but this pierces the soul and inward affections. Then was I assuredly persuaded that I should not die till I had preached Christ Jesus where I now am (Edinburgh, in St Giles). And yet, having now my hearty desire, I am nothing satisfied, neither rejoice. My God, remove my unthankfulness.

However in less than a month he was writing to her: 'We have had a wonderful experience of God's merciful providence'. The change in fortune came after a series of military setbacks for the Congregation despite the efforts of Lord James Stewart and Arran as field commanders. D'Oysel had taken Stirling and had driven back the forces of the Congregation into Fife, where it looked as if he was going to mop them up. Knox had offered his services to rally the troops but they were declined after an incident in Fife, when his sermon on Jehoshaphat (who always showed himself to his troops) was taken amiss by young Arran, who tended to hold himself aloof in his tent. It was suggested to Knox that if he was going to offend the Hamiltons it was better that he did not preach at all, or as Knox himself put it in a letter (January 29): 'I am judged amongst ourselves too extreme and by reason thereof I have extracted myself from all public assemblies to my private study.' Thus when the end came, Knox could only take pleasure as a spectator.

The decisive element was the winter weather. The French fleet had set out at last in late December with 4,500 troops under the command of another Guise, the Marquis d'Elboeuf, but storms blew most of them ashore in Flanders. At the same time Elizabeth had unleashed her forces northwards with instructions to annoy the French as much as possible and if necessary claim they were acting on their own initiative (an interesting reversal of Cecil's rebuke to Knox when he had suggested as much). Of the fourteen English ships which left Gillingham on December 27 under Admiral Winter, eight sailed into the Forth on January 22. They were just in time to cut d'Oysel's lines of communication to the Queen Regent across the Firth of Forth in Leith. The timely English initiative was followed by the Treaty of Berwick, which was signed with the lords of the Congregation in February. It guaranteed the Scots help in their desire to be 'loyal to their Queen' and to be free of French domination. Shortly thereafter an English force of 9,000 soldiers closed on the French at Leith. Mary of Guise, who was now weak in health and dying, retired to the neutrality of Edinburgh Castle (still held by Erskine) and was visited there by Willock and Lord James. In April 1560 Knox was back in his pulpit in St Giles, and down the hill over 10,000 French and English troops faced each other on the south side of the river Forth. The fate of Scotland was to be decided by England, France and Spain, the three signatories to the Peace of Cateau-Cambresis a year previously, which had put an end to the perennial wars between them. All three countries now had incentives to end the civil war in Scotland.

The inaction of France and England was partly explained because both countries were short of funds with which to support expeditionary forces. In March France acquired additional problems at home when French Protestants attempted (through the conspiracy of Amboise) to overthrow the Guises and the Cardinal of Lorraine. The attempt was suppressed but there was still a risk of civil war over the question of religious freedom and the French were reluctant to over-commit themselves in Scotland, especially as it would involve them indirectly against England. In a bold initiative, therefore, they invited their old enemy and new ally, Spain, to assist them in supressing heresy in Scotland.

Much as Philip II was zealous in his wish to uphold the Catholic faith, he perceived that if he helped the French to annexe Scotland it would enable them to invade England more easily. They would then control the English Channel, so denying Spain access to their ports in the Low Countries. Philip entertained the idea of sending a force himself to Scotland and raised 4,400 mercenaries in the Netherlands. It would have been a devastating blow for the Congregation in Scotland had this scheme progressed further. But the Duke of Alva persuaded him that it was better to let the French stew in their own Scottish mess; and when a Spanish fleet was destroyed by the Turks in North Africa, Philip dropped the plan and ordered his force to sail south [Ridley, pp. 374–5]. Elizabeth immediately opened negotiations with the French, and considered abandoning the Scots. She did not want a costly war with France but was angry that Mary Queen of Scots included the English arms in her coat of arms, and was only too well aware that a French triumph in Scotland could topple her crown.

The French were thus obliged to settle with the English and on July 6 1560 the Treaty of Edinburgh was signed, under which all French troops were withdrawn from Scotland and the question of a religious settlement was referred to a Scottish Parliament. Knox had his victory. He delivered a thanksgiving sermon in St Giles, in which he gave the victory to God, and a prayer in which he said:

Seeing that thou hast made our confederates of England the instruments by whom we are now set at this liberty to whom we in thy name have promised mutual faith again, let us never fall to that unkindness, O Lord, that either we declare ourselves unthankful unto them, or profaners of thy holy name.

He had not lost hope of acceptance by England, but it was never to be.

The Treaty of Edinburgh had left Scotland in a curious position. It affirmed not only the sovereignty of the King and Queen of France, but also the rights of a Scottish Church and the role of England as guardian of 'old freedoms and liberties from conquest'. It seemed at first sight that both Knox's dreams of a religious revolution, establishing his brand of protestantism and the expulsion of the French, had become a reality. But had they? In the sixteenth century the settlement of religion obviously had to be something to which the sovereign agreed and the Scottish sovereign Mary was busy sending her ambassador to Rome to offer obedience to the newly-elected Pope Pius IV. Her husband, Francis, having offered his obedience to the new pope, was preparing to crack down on the Huguenot Protestants in France. This was hardly the attitude of a queen and king of a Protestant country.

The position of the surviving Roman Church in Scotland was anomalous, to say the least. Its clergy still had the right to sit in any Parliament empowered to decide the question of religious settlement. However there were only a few of them around to cast their votes. Of the thirteen Scottish dioceses, five were vacant; one had a layman (another of James V's illegitimate sons) as its bishop; the Archbishop of Glasgow had fled with the French troops, taking his treasure with him; two others had turned Protestant and a third was about to do so. That left three prelates, whose morals as well as theology were decidedly pre-Reformation. All these men still had the right and title to the church's income and wealth.

The Pope, about to launch a new session of the Council of Trent, was hardly going to let the matter lie. Nor was he going to appoint men who would make a settlement with Knox and allow Scotland to make its own Reformation. When Mary Queen of Scots made it clear that she was not going to ratify the Treaty of Edinburgh, the English and the lords of the Congregation acted quickly together to come up with solutions. The English ambassador was urging the Scots to follow the English model and forge the new church out of the old. For their part the lords were also prepared to ignore the Treaty of Edinburgh, and were working for the marriage of Chatelherault's son Arran to Elizabeth of England. This match, had it prospered, would have resulted in a union of the Scottish and English crowns fifty years earlier than actually happened, and consequently the absorption of Scottish religion into the Anglican Church before it had a chance to be established and confirmed in the form which Knox and his colleagues had conceived. It did not happen, because Elizabeth was not interested in a marriage with Arran.

The first irony was that John Knox, who all along had been well-disposed to England from religious, emotional and political motives, and supported the idea of Arran's marrying Elizabeth, would soon have been silenced had such a move ever taken place. The second irony was that by continuing to work for his ideals he helped to prevent it happening.

Knox and the other five Johns had not been idle in the previous months. They had been preparing the Scots Confession and the First Book of Discipline. The former was broadly similar to that of the French Protestant Church and was Calvinistic in theology, and stressed the authority of the Bible in all matters. The latter was a much more ambitious project, similar in aim to Calvin's Institutes: it set out a vision of a church and society working in harmony, a kind of spiritual welfare state. The most radical and unique part (with which Knox is generally credited) was the section which sought to use the patrimony of the Old Church to set up a system by which every child would have a right to education up to a minimum level. It even drafted a syllabus for the universities which was both relevant and modern, substituting subjects like economics and physics for some of the scholastic disciplines required for ministers. Had it been accepted it would have made this small and somewhat uncultivated nation a leader in European educational practice. Of course it required the lords to give up their share of the Old Church's spoils, and that is where its problems began and ended.

The preachers were anxious to have their religious settlement and approached the Parliament that was due to meet in August

1560 with three demands: to abolish 'idolatrous' practices; to find a remedy for the discipline of a new church; and to abolish the right of the Pope to derive income from the church or his representatives to have a seat in the legislature. The Parliament of the Three Estates (which included Archbishop Hamilton and the Old Church but not Knox or his colleagues) agreed to the first demand and asked the preachers to furnish a Confession upon which any new church under the second demand would be founded. This was quickly done. The Scots Confession was amended and brought forward. Amended, because weeks afterwards the English ambassador Randolph wrote to Cecil saying he was glad that the section on obedience to the civil magistrate had been omitted. Reading between the lines we can imagine that Knox had included some of the revolutionary thinking which had fuelled his vision during the previous years and which his colleagues persuaded him to drop in order to win the day. The Scots Parliament, with the Catholic bishops abstaining and only a couple of votes against, passed the Confession, and on August 17 1560 Scotland became officially a Protestant state, with the mass outlawed and the papacy's jurisdiction denied.

This was the hour of victory but it was not total. The third demand of the preachers had only been partly met. The Third Estate remained as part of the realm, which meant the Old Church was still partly recognised by the state. It had lost the right to raise revenues but these were not assigned to the new church and so there was no money with which to establish the framework of a new religion. The Book of Discipline was still unapproved and without a constitution no church could hope to be legally and practically established.

The difference between the English and Scottish Reformations can be seen distinctly at this moment of birth of the new deal in Scotland. England vested its monarch with all the rights and prerogatives removed from the Pope. Scotland annulled these powers altogether. England prescribed the use of an official form of public worship (the Cranmer Prayer Book), whereas Scotland proscribed the mass. England accepted the machinery of the Catholic Church, whereas Scotland left open the question of how the church would be governed.

The lack of a detailed charter for the new church at this point had some advantages. It is clear from a study of the lairds who attended the Reformation Parliament that it was packed with those from Protestant areas. The new religion was still in the minority and did not yet have enough popular support throughout Scotland to be adopted as the uniform faith of the nation. It left room for compromises and left the door open for the preachers to persuade the nobility to assign them a sufficient proportion of the Old Church's revenues to be able to carry out their plans for a new established church.

It also had one major disadvantage, which Knox himself acknowledges in his account of the Treaty of Edinburgh. He frankly admits that the Queen's representatives had left the Articles of Religion to be decided by their Majesties. When the Queen's representative, Sir James Sandilands, laid before Mary and Francis the results of the 1560 Reformation Parliament, the Queen flatly refused to endorse them. Without the royal assent, any religious settlement was a precarious one, as Knox was only too well aware. He was also hearing from his French contacts that after the uprising in Lyons the Guises had moved in to crush the Huguenots, and the hangmen were assembling to deal with their leaders including the Prince of Condé, brother of Antoine, King of Navarre. There were rumours that once the Guises had mopped up in their own backyard they would repudiate the Treaty of Edinburgh and invade Scotland again.

It was against this background that the first General Assembly of the new church met in Edinburgh on December 20 1560, consisting of forty-one people, six of whom were ministers. For John Knox this ought to have been his hour of triumph, but it was overshadowed by two deaths which were to disturb his peace in very different ways. The first was that of his wife Marjory, whose sudden demise left him 'in no small heaviness'. The second was equally sudden and occurred far away in France. Through his Huguenot friends he was the first in Scotland to know that Francis II, King of France and Scotland, had died. Scotland now had an eighteen-year-old widow Queen. Knox hurried through the dark *vennel* which led from his house in Trunk's Close, round to the Hamilton family residence at the Kirk o'Field (the present site of Edinburgh University quad), where he found Lord James

Stewart and Chatelherault. At first they would not believe the rumour but it was soon confirmed. The two lords agreed that as soon as possible a Parliament of the Three Estates should be summoned for January 1561.

The failure of Queen Mary to endorse the religious settlement of 1560 has been adduced as evidence that it was never legally or constitutionally approved. The Scottish Parliament of 1567 ratified the Acts of 1560, but those who dispute their legality usually take the view that this Parliament sat under the regency of the Earl of Moray, who had obtained the abdication of Queen Mary by force, and that it was therefore itself invalid. Knox in turn has been accused of being economical with the truth in his account of the refusal of Francis and Mary to ratify the Acts concerning religion, since he assumes their refusal was part of a general policy not to ratify anything, and was of little practical significance. The year 1560 with its three key events (the Treaty of Edinburgh, the Reformation Parliament, and the first General Assembly) represents the fulcrum-point of Scotland's history, and so it is worth considering whether the settlement was justly obtained.

Knox was in no doubt that it was. He contended that it was not the fault of the Protestants that the Queen had absented herself from Scotland, and that in her absence the Estates had full legal power to assemble Parliament. Moreover he argued that the Parliament of 1560 was more lawful and free than any for a hundred years, since the votes of men were free and given of conscience. This is slightly disingenuous, since there is evidence that many of the Catholic landowners stayed away from the 1560 Parliament. However it is also true to say that those who attended were not coerced and its decisions represented general opinion throughout Scotland that the time was ripe to discard the old system and embrace the new.

Perhaps the legality of the proceedings can best be decided by the maxim that revolutions are a law unto themselves. If there is any question mark above the events of 1560, it should ask how such fundamental changes could have been achieved so peacefully within the framework of the Constitution. The fact that they were makes the revolution of 1560 all the more remarkable.

13

Double-Crossed Vision

The spiritual welfare state envisaged by Knox was never to materialise. It might seem optimistic to think that it could ever have become a reality. The six Johns considered the precedent of England, where, although Henry VIII had stripped many of the religious houses of their assets, the resources of the secular clergy were still available for the most part to the new church. In Scotland a deal was struck that those who had held, or had appropriated church revenue could keep two-thirds and the remaining third would be divided between the church and the Crown. Knox put it more colourfully: 'two parts freely given to the devil and the third divided betwixt God and the devil'. He added the prediction that it would not be long before the devil had three-thirds and asked his audience to guess what the church's share then would be. His prediction was to prove only too accurate.

However as the Reformers began their task the opportunity for Scotland to start afresh did still seem attainable. Across the North Sea in Germany Frederick, Elector of Saxony, had apportioned the church revenues for the threefold purpose of caring for the poor, funding education, and providing ministers for the church. That was precisely what the First Book of Discipline proposed to do in Scotland. What actually happened in Scotland was that the Old Church (despite its mass being outlawed) could still legally draw ecclesiastical income, as could the lords and lay commendators. There was little left over to fund the structure of a spiritual welfare state.

This is one of the tragedies of Scottish history, far more important than the host of battles that were lost or won on Scottish soil and which have found their way into the anthems of posterity. In this short and remarkably clear manifesto is a social charter which would have vaulted Scotland to the forefront of humanitarian reform in Europe. It was no pallid copy of Geneva or crib of the Lutheran states. As we have seen, the Book of Discipline laid great emphasis on a national education system. It envisaged providing a school in every parish in which there would be a teacher qualified to teach Latin. No child would be prevented by poverty from attending and a system of bursaries would enable them to go to university. When they reached university there would be no question of studying the Bible through the opaque glass of scholastic theology or Latin versions: Greek and Hebrew would enable the minister to study it in the original tongue, while each family head would be expected to read the Bible to his family in the common tongue. It can be called theocratic or democratic, but it was revolutionary none the less. Here was a Reform movement not only supported by the common people, but which could be sustained by them as they took advantage of the education reforms.

Equally important, the Book of Discipline provided for the poor. In the sixteenth century the provisions of its fifth section were far-reaching and visionary:

We are not patrons for stubborn and idle beggars who, running from place to place, make a craft of their begging, whom the Civil magistrate ought to punish; but for the widow and the fatherless, the aged impotent or lamed, who neither can nor may travail for their sustenation, we say that God commandeth his people to be careful. And therefore for such, as also for persons of honesty fallen into decay and penury, ought such provision be made that of our abundance their indigence be relieved. How this most conveniently and most easily be done in every city and other parts of this Realm, God shall show the wisdom and means, so that your minds be godly thereto inclined.

Those who criticise the creation in Scotland of church courts for moral offences as oppressively punitive are compelled to deal with the historical reality: namely that the powers of the counter-Reformation countries elsewhere in Europe, in their zeal to see Scotland return to catholicism, would have burnt any of the authors of the Book of Discipline as heretics. In these countries there was no attempt to right the kinds of injustice which had flowed from the patrimony system. Before we condemn Knox and his brethren for the violence of the language in the opening section, in which they inveigh against idolatrous religion, or indict them as intolerant of moral misdemeanours, we should remember that there was no such thing as tolerance of religion in the sixteenth century. Previously there had been but one model to which all were required to conform. The prevailing assumption was that the only way that the church state equilibrium could be maintained was to replace one monopoly with another one. That the 'ane haly kirk' of the Scots Reformers was a better and more just system than the one it replaced, there is no doubt. Whether it should then have been reconciled to a purified Roman Catholic system is only a theoretical question. The Counter-Reformation had widened the gap. By the mid-sixteenth century the two systems were incompatible and it was a matter of choosing which one better represented the truth.

The rest of the Book of Discipline is mostly concerned with the polity of the church. Its worship was based on the Geneva service book and although the infrequent, quarterly communions may have been of necessity dictated by the shortage of ministers, there was no Prayer Book in the Anglican sense or canon of the communion service as in the mass. The ministry of the new church was to be composed of ministers, deacons and elders. These were to be elected and strict conditions for the qualification of ministers were applied. The Reformers did not want to see an influx into the new church of unemployed priests and other time-servers who did not share the beliefs they had fought so hard to secure. In addition there were to be ten superintendents, three fewer than the number of Scottish bishops in the Old Church. Much presbyterian sweat has been expended in arguing about the office of superintendent and the size of his stipend (five times that of a minister). Some have argued that these superintendents were bishops in effect and others that they were nothing of the kind, being elected to serve an area rather than to 'rule' it. The debate has been clouded by the fact that bishops were introduced into the Church of Scotland after Knox's death in an attempt by James VI to subjugate the church to the monarchy, and they became a hated company. Suffice it to say that Knox's superintendents were not bishops as we would recognise them, then or now. Although the scheme was formally adopted, the superintendents never really had a chance to prove themselves before the controversy over bishops engulfed the kirk. Knox himself declined to be one, preferring to settle for his pulpit in St Giles.

The failure of the Book of Discipline to be immediately ratified meant that, with a shortage of ministers and funds, the church had to rely on 'readers' (lay preachers), who were paid a mere fraction of a minister's salary of £120 to supply the spiritual needs of the 1,000 churches which came into being in the first decade of the Reformation. The ideal of democracy contained in the system of Kirk Sessions at parish level was seriously handicapped by the generally low level of Scots education (which it was attempting to remedy). Instead of godly, cottage patriarchs dispensing discipline in the Kirk Session, there tended to be an élite who emerged by virtue of their education and skills, and this made it more difficult for the new church to fulfil its aim – to be truly a church of the people. Scholars have picked over the changes and modifications made in the Book of Discipline during its gestation and there have been suggestions that it was Willock, not Knox, who drafted certain key sections. Be that as it may, the matter is of academic interest only, as the book was destined to be blocked. It was too radical and too visionary for the kind of men who were running Scotland at the time. In January 1561 they signed their names to it, but it was a cynical ploy to buy time and the six Johns were out-manoeuvred. The Scottish nobility chose a queen instead of a constitution.

Although the Reformation Parliament of August 1560 had adopted the Confession, this had still not been ratified by Queen Mary. Knox was well aware – as he says in his account of the Treaty of Edinburgh – that matters of the religious settlement were ultimately to be decided by the sovereign. The need was all the more pressing to put a church system in place and present Mary with a *fait accompli*. Some of the lords had other priorities, and the Catholic nobility of the north-east were determined to get to their new Queen and influence her to come to Scotland on a counter-Reformation crusade. The emissary of the Gordons of Huntly, John Leslie, was sent to Paris to persuade Mary to take ship to Aberdeen, raise an army there and march on Edinburgh. She rightly rejected this inept advice. Instead the ambassador of the Great Council, Lord James Stewart, her half-brother whom she knew and trusted, persuaded her to return to Scotland with her own retinue. He reassured her that she could bring with her the ways of the French court if she wished, which would encourage among the nobility a sophistication that was lacking in Scottish life and perhaps even raise the prestige of the country in Europe. Yes, she could even continue to hear the Catholic mass, but of course it would be a private affair.

Mary wanted to know if John Knox would raise a revolution against her. She had read the First Blast and had sent a copy to Elizabeth of England. Lord James reassured Mary and produced an undertaking which he had obtained from Knox. He did not tell her that Knox had insisted that there was to be no question of giving in on the issue of the mass. We know about these exchanges through Throckmorton, the English ambassador to France, who wrote to Cecil on March 20 1561: 'Mr Knox in certain articles given to my Lord James at this time hath mitigated somewhat the rigour of his book, referring much unto the time that the same was written.' Throckmorton urged Queen Elizabeth not to forget how useful Knox continued to be for English purposes. 'I take him to be as much for your purpose as any man of all that nation, and that his doing therein, and his zeal, sufficiently recompense his fault in writing that book, and therefore he is not to be driven out of that realm.'

It is clear, before they ever met, that Mary Queen of Scots and John Knox more feared than admired one another. Distance did not lend enchantment but rather the opposite. The images they seemed to have of one another have sometimes been taken up by their supporters. Knox was no more a domineering old curmudgeon, trampling roughshod over this sensitive and lonely spirit, torturing her with his vials of wrath, than she was a luckless and fragile angel in pink sugar. Dismissing these overblown caricatures brings us to several possible views of Mary. First she was only eighteen years of age and had very little experience of Scotland except what she had learned at the French court. There she seems to have absorbed a French model of monarchy and no doubt something of the Guise ambition. The belief that she was the rightful Queen of England as well as Scotland seems to have been firmly planted in her head. How then do we interpret her subsequent actions? Was she the champion of royal absolutism, forced by the divided kingdom to disguise her true colours but working secretly for the triumph of the monarchy and its restoration? Was she the staunch Catholic loyal to the Pope and determined to see the true church restored to her native land; or the heroine who by feminine charm managed to unite the warring nobility and yet fell victim through the weakness of the heart to the venal ambitions of others?

She was, I suspect, none of these things, but has been painted as such by her many biographers. The best of these contrasting views of Mary Queen of Scots can be seen in the sympathetic portrait by Antonia Fraser and the unsympathetic character-analysis by Jenny Wormwald. Yet Mary has had more than her share of the limelight at this highly dramatic moment in Scottish history, and so we should inquire whether or not Knox's reaction to her was a just one. It is not necessary to come to a final view of the Queen or even to look for consistency in her policies. One thing that can be asserted, however, is that her position was not impossible or untenable. What we can judge is whether she made it so by her actions. Knox certainly made one error about Mary. He attributed to her his own deep concern for religion and its place within the state. As Hugh Watt remarks:

He did not know that this chosen vessel of the counter-Reformation was at heart a child of the Renaissance. Picturing her as a devotee, he was unaware that colour, gaiety and romance, love and power meant more to her than Church or religion and that . . . there would always be some ploy of her own.

Watt sees her dream of marrying Don Carlos of Spain as her dearest ploy. Eustace Percy remarks that she had a compulsion to marry because 'marriage was an essential protection; yet the ruinous spoilt boy (Darnley) she married was almost the best of her seven suitors; of the other six, three (Young Arran, Eric of Sweden and Carlos of Spain) were mental defectives; Robert Dudley was a sister-queen's discarded favourite'. That left the Archduke of Austria and Charles IX of France, who were never practical propositions. The trouble with being a child of the Renaissance in 1561 was that the spirit of the Renaissance had died in the Habsburg-Valois wars a generation earlier.

Elizabeth balked at the thought of her rival travelling to Scotland through England and perhaps exciting sympathy, so Mary was compelled to land at Leith on Tuesday, August 19 1561. Knox took the bad weather as a portent of 'dolour, darkness and all impiety'. The Queen took up residence in Holyrood Palace, whose royal apartments can be toured today and a sense of the ambience in which she lived may be absorbed. It was a darker and colder climate than she had been used to. Above Holyrood broods Arthur's Seat and the Salisbury Crags, and to the west the Royal Mile slopes gently upwards through the old town of Edinburgh, where Knox lived and preached, to the fortress of Edinburgh Castle, where Erskine's giant cannon had kept watch throughout the siege of Leith.

The first week went well. Everyone seemed impressed, except Knox. Randolph, the English ambassador, noted to his dismay that Knox did not even seem to be giving the Queen a chance: '(He) thundereth out of the pulpit and I fear nothing so much that one day he will mar all. He ruleth the roost, and of him all men stand in fear.' On the Queen's first Sunday in Scotland a French priest said mass in her private chapel and Lord James had to bar the door against protesters, who would have been unaware of the terms he had negotiated and were determined to stop it. The next day Queen Mary and her council issued a proclamation which, in the absence of royal endorsement of the settlement of religion reached by the Scots Parliament, was the only constitutional ruling on religious questions. The edict stated that no liege on pain of death was to make any alteration or innovation in the religion 'Her Majesty found public and universally standing at Her Majesty's arrival'. The ambiguity was no doubt deliberate. A protective shield not only covered the Congregation but insulated the royal household and gave it the right to attend mass as part of the accepted practice. Knox was furious. Arran protested, but Lord James had cut the Hamiltons out of the court circle and he went unheard.

It may seem churlish on Knox's part to deny Mary the religion she had grown up with, but he was being consistent. If he compromised now, what chance was there of getting a new Scottish Church set up in law? He mounted the pulpit the next Sunday and uttered the famous words: 'One mass is more fearful to me than if ten thousand armies were landed in any part of the realm, of purpose to suppress the whole religion.'

He had thrown down the gauntlet and the Queen quickly picked it up. Knox was summoned to Holyrood that week and ushered into a room where he was confronted by Lord James and the Queen. The account of the meeting is given in detail in Knox's *History*, Book IV [Dickinson, II, 13ff], and while we must allow that Knox gave himself the verdict in the contest, his integrity as a recorder has not been seriously challenged on this and subsequent encounters, and his skill as a dramatist is certainly revealed.

We take up the story after Knox has dealt with Mary's opening accusation that he had fomented rebellion against her mother and was the author of the First Blast. The Queen asked him straight out, 'Think ye that subjects having power may resist their princes?' Knox replied:

If the princes exceed their powers, Madam, and do that wherefore they should not be obeyed, it is no doubt but they may be resisted even by power. For there is neither greater honour nor greater obedience to be given to kings or princes, than God has commanded to be given to father and mother. But so it is, Madam, that the father may be stricken with a frenzy, in the which he would slay his own children. Now, Madam, if the children arise, join themselves together, apprehend the father, take the sword and other weapons from him, and finally bind his hands and keep him in prison till his frenzy be past; think ye, Madam, that the children do wrong? Or think ye, Madam, that God will be offended with them that have stayed their father to commit wickedness? It is even so with princes that would murder the children of God that are subject unto them. Their blind zeal is nothing but a mad frenzy; and therefore to take the sword from them, to bind their hands and to cast themselves in prison till they be brought to a more sober mind, is no disobedience against princes but just obedience, because it agrees with the will of God.

Mary was stunned at this pointed parable. Lord James saw her face change and asked if something had offended her. After a long pause she said: 'Well, then, I perceive that my subjects shall obey you and not me; and shall do what they list, and not what I command: and so I must be subject to them and not them to me.' Knox's reply shows that he could be diplomatic. He said in effect, God forbid that he should want to command anyone to obey him, since it is the princes and their subjects who are both to obey God but the former are given the role of foster parent to the church, and the latter are not bound to follow the religion of their princes, but this God-given guardianship is the greatest vocation that anyone could wish for. Mary retorted, 'But ye are not the Kirk that I will nourish. I will defend the Kirk of Rome for I think that it is the true Kirk of God.'

'Your will is no reason, Madam,' countered Knox. 'Neither doth your thought make the Roman harlot to be the true and immaculate spouse of Jesus Christ.' He offered to prove, as in his first sermon at St Andrews, how much the Catholic Church had degenerated from the purity of the apostolic era. The Queen calmly replied, 'My conscience says that is not so.' Knox rounded on her, 'Conscience requires knowledge and I fear the right knowledge ye have none.' She immediately rapped back, 'But I have both heard and read.' Knox countered that this was not good enough since the Jews who crucified Jesus had read both the law and the prophets. Well, rejoined Mary, how can anyone settle the matter, since Knox and his brethren interpreted the Scriptures their way – and who would then judge? Scripture, said Knox, and introduced his favourite topic, the mass, the issue which had brought about the meeting. Mass is nowhere commanded nor authorised in the Scriptures, Knox argued. Mary retorted that if Catholic theologians were present they would answer him. Knox was clearly confident that he would be able to have the best of it and that the papists would not dispute the issue, but Mary replied that he might have the chance to defend his position sooner than he anticipated.

Recognising that the interview was getting nowhere, she excused herself to go to dinner. Knox took the opportunity at the end of his first audience to hope that the Queen might be 'as blessed within the Commonwealth of Scotland, if it be the pleasure of God, as ever Deborah was in the Commonwealth of Israel'. Bearing in mind his somewhat ambiguous attitude to Deborah as an exception to the rule, this is heavy irony. Thus ended round one.

Even allowing for special pleading in Knox's reporting of the incident, he gives enough of the argument to show the clash of two opposing ideologies. His own verdict on Mary after that first encounter shows that he had respect for his adversary: 'If there be not in her a proud mind, a crafty wit and an indurate heart against God and his truth, my judgment faileth me.' His verdict was confirmed for him when in October Mary laid aside an order of the Edinburgh Burgh Council which expelled all whoremongers and papists from the town. (At that time, Edinburgh consisted of the upper end of the Royal Mile; the lower end was a separate area called Canongate in which Holyrood Palace lay.) The Queen dismissed the Provost and baillies, declaring that Edinburgh must be open to all her subjects. It was not an unreasonable stance, but it confirmed the suspicions of the Congregation that when they did anything to confirm the status of their religious settlement, she would overturn it. Writing to Cecil at the time, Knox declared, 'Her whole proceedings do declare that the cardinal's lessons are so deeply printed in her heart that the substance and the qualities are like to perish together. I would be glad to be deceived but I fear I shall not' [*Works*; Laing, VI, 132].

During this period Edinburgh was a town of about 12,500 souls, and was larger than Zurich or Geneva. The Canongate

Above: A view of St Andrews from the top of St Rule's Tower in the Cathedral grounds. The Castle ruins can be seen centre right, and St Salvator's Tower centre left.

Left: John Knox's pulpit, originally in Holy Trinity Church, St Andrews, but now housed across the road in St Salvator's Chapel.

Portrait of Mary, Queen of Scots.

James Stewart, Earl of Moray.

Above: John Knox House in Edinburgh's Royal Mile, now open to the public as a museum.

Left: Statue of John Knox, outside the General Assembly Hall in Edinburgh.

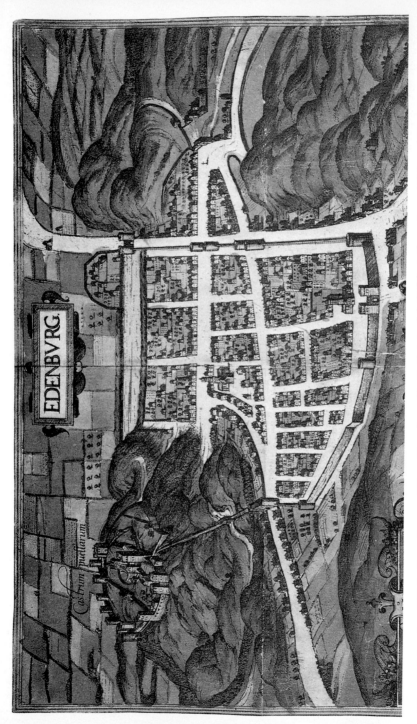

EDENBVRG.

Castrum puellarum

Plan of Edinburgh, c. 1582, by Georg Braun and Franz Hogenburg. The Castle is top left, St Giles in the centre and Holyrood House at extreme centre right.

additionally had a population of over 2,000. Michael Lynch's study concludes that even as late as 1565 there was not a Protestant majority in the city. Although Knox had a majority of supporters among the baillies, not all the Protestants were of unalloyed zeal. The leaders were a 'curious collection of conservatives, trimmers and activists' [Lynch, p. 188]. Among the first two categories (as Maitland of Lethington admitted to Cecil in August 1561) were the covetous, the complacent and the inconstant who were liable to be overawed by the royal court. It was the last category that was worrying Knox. Although a system of communion tokens had been set up by which attendance at church could be checked (1,300 attended at Easter 1561), a great number of crypto-Catholics and the numbers sneaking into Holyrood for mass were exaggerated by both sides, one from fear and the other for propaganda.

The port of Leith, which prior to 1560 had been a channel for Protestant ideas to enter Edinburgh, now became the mirror image, the conduit by which continental catholicism could enter Scotland. Knox became depressed and wrote to Calvin as the only person 'to whom I can confide my anxieties . . . I never before felt how weighty and difficult a matter it is to contend against hypocrisy under the guise of piety' [October 24 1561]. There is no record of any reply and we may perhaps conclude that Calvin once again adhered to his doctrine of loyalty to princes.

Knox felt betrayed by Lord James and Lethington, both of whom seemed to have abandoned the preachers in a new strategy of winning over Mary. Knox saw this as plain and simple appeasement. Lethington was a clever opportunist who was annoyed by what he saw as Knox's unsophisticated approach. When the Book of Discipline was presented to the Privy Council at the end of 1561, it was Lethington who undermined it by suggesting that those nobles who had signed it would not be willing to put it into practice. He was working for a political and religious settlement which would be on the old monarchical lines and as such was utterly incompatible with the settlement that Knox desired. The Book of Discipline, on which Knox had pinned his hopes, was shelved.

14

Counter-Reformation

1562 was the year in which the Roman Catholics of Scotland grew more confident. Knox went preaching in the autumn in the south-west and found himself challenged to public debate by Quintin Kennedy, the Abbot of Crossraguel in Ayrshire. Kennedy was around Knox's age and a shrewd tactician. Much fencing took place about the venue of the debate and how many should be present as witnesses and recorders. Kennedy won the choice of the Collegiate Church of Maybole and Knox in turn won his demand for a written record. It was just as well he did since the Abbot acquitted himself so well that the impression got around that he had won on points, forcing Knox to publish the disputation to put the record straight. The subject of the debate was the mass.

The event aroused great interest and was undoubtedly a dramatic occasion. Whether or not it proved anything is open to doubt since the argument turned around Kennedy's assertion that the example of the Old Testament priest Melchizedek, who used bread and wine at the altar, was the scriptural justification for applying this to the Lord's Supper. It took the battle on to Knox's own ground, since he was fond (some might say over-fond) of Old Testament allusion. Kennedy was clever enough to concede that the sacrifice of the cross was unique and not repeated by a priest. He contended that the sacrifice of the mass was one of commemoration of Christ's death and passion. Knox's answer was that there was no sacrifice in the mass since the one and only act of sacrifice had been made on the cross and if there was only commemoration in the Lord's Supper it was therefore not a sacrifice. They seemed to be getting bogged down in semantics until Knox got on to transubstantiation.

Knox advanced the argument that if the bread of the Host was truly the real body of Christ as in the mass, it would make God prey to rats and mice who could nibble him. What is important is that the debate was perceived by Roman Catholics as a victory for Kennedy and gave them confidence that at last the dominant position of the Protestants in the intellectual debate was being shaken.

Knox also had another terrier snapping at his heels in the person of Ninian Winzet of Linlithgow, who challenged him to define how he derived his authority within the church. Knox did not choose to respond to the challenge, preferring to take side-swipes from his pulpit in St Giles's. When Winzet published a mocking pamphlet entitled *The Last Blast of the Trumpet of God's word against the usurped authority of John Knox and his Calvinian Brethren Intruded preachers*, the Edinburgh Council had it seized. Winzet left Scotland for Europe where he directed further attacks at the new kirk from a distance.

An even more pungent attack on Knox (eventually published in 1581 in Paris) was Nicol Burne's *Disputation concerning the Controversed heads of Religion*, which demonstrates that the Protestants had no monopoly of name-calling. Burne alleges that Knox was committing incest with his mother-in-law and was in league with the devil, full of lusts and a 'decrepit old man'. Those who had a low opinion of the Reformers were handed further ammunition in 1562 when the Reformed Church suffered a public scandal. One of its ministers, Paul Methven of Jedburgh, a friend of Knox, was found guilty of adultery and deposed from the ministry.

In Europe the counter-Reformation was in full swing. Jesuit envoys came secretly to Scotland where they observed the effects of Knoxian religion and were given an audience by the Queen. They delivered a letter from the Pope urging her to follow the example of Mary Tudor. Intelligence of their presence had been passed to Knox and he used the Jesuits' visit to 'rage wonderfully' at the 'papist plot'. Knox's fear that the gains made by the Protestants could easily be swept aside were compounded by examples which he saw all around of 'revisionist' practices.

He is often thought to have held utterly puritanical views on dancing, but to the no-frills, lower-class Scot the masques which the Queen held at Holyrood were excessively extravagant at a time of budget deficits for the Crown, and poverty for the new church. They were an excuse for the kind of frivolity delighted in by the Queen's inner coterie of ladies-in-waiting, the four Marys or 'Maries' (Livingstone, Beaton, Fleming and Seton). Knox does not appear to have been particularly severe on dancing until, in December 1562 at the close of this year of setbacks, he had more bad news from France where nearly 800 Scots Protestant volunteers had been wiped out when the Duke of Guise suppressed the Huguenots in Rouen. Shortly afterwards there was a roisterous ball at Holyrood and Knox got it into his head that this was some kind of celebration for the Rouen massacre. He let fly in the pulpit next Sunday and very soon afterwards received his second invitation to Holyrood Palace.

Lord James was there again; he was now further in Mary's favour, since he had led the expedition earlier in the year to crush a revolt by the Earl of Huntly. (Huntly, who was mentally unstable, seems to have been one of the long line of men who were fatally attracted to Mary but also determined to 'tame' her.) Knox had conducted Lord James's wedding in the February of that year but was becoming wary of his loyalty to the cause. He had more reason to be suspicious of Lethington, who was also present at his audience in the Queen's bedchamber. The gist of the Queen's complaint was quickly put. If in future Knox had anything to take issue with her, he should come to her personally and tell her and she would hear him.

Knox sensed danger. He was not being offered a position as a court preacher akin to the role he had enjoyed in England but Mary was trying to buy him off in precisely the way that she had bought off these two lords of the Congregation. He knew that no one within the Queen's court circle would take heed of what he had to say. What would he lose in respect and following among the brethren if it was known, as it would be, that he was whispering in the Queen's ear? His reply to Mary as written down later was probably ruder than when delivered:

I will most gladly wait upon your Grace's pleasure, time and place. But to wait upon your chamber door, or elsewhere and then to have no further liberty but to whisper my mind in your Grace's ear, or to tell you what others think or speak of you, neither will my conscience nor the vocation whereto God hath called me, suffer it. For albeit I am at your Grace's command here now, yet I cannot tell what other men shall judge of me, that at this time of day I am absent from my book and waiting upon the court.

'You will not always be at your book,' said Mary and turned her back on him, the interview at an end. When others remarked that he appeared unshaken by this interview, and showed no fear, Knox replied, 'Why should the pleasing face of a gentlewoman effray me? I have looked on the faces of angry men and yet not been afraid above measure.' Today he would be called a sexist. In sixteenth-century terms he was no courtier either.

That interview took place on December 15 1562. During the next few months Knox grew increasingly frustrated at the lack of any further progress by Parliament on the matter of religion. Then on Easter Sunday (April 11 1563) the leading Catholic clergy grew bolder and celebrated the mass publicly in Ayr. The Protestant lairds of Ayrshire arrested them, including the Archbishop of St Andrews, John Hamilton, and demanded that the 1560 law forbidding the mass be upheld. Mary sent for Knox. This time the setting for their meeting was in Kinross at the picturesque castle of Loch Leven to the east of the route north from Edinburgh to Perth. Throughout the year the loch changes mood to reflect the weather over Fife, to the east. The weather is not recorded for their interview on April 13 but Mary's mood was reconciliatory. She must have been aware of the rising sectarian temperature in Scotland as her own musicians had refused to play for her mass on Christmas day, probably because they feared attack from Protestant mobs. She knew of the arrests in Ayrshire and she asked Knox to intervene to prevent the punishment of the Catholic clergy, since they were simply practising the religion they believed in. Knox predictably replied that the law must be enforced and the mass had been

outlawed. She pleaded with him for two hours to do something
to avoid anarchy. 'Will you allow that they should take my sword
in their hand?' she asked, a clear hint that unless he complied,
she would use force. Knox replied, 'The sword of justice is
God's and if princes and rulers fail to use it, others may.' He
refused to interfere and the Queen retired to supper, Knox to
a bedroom in the castle where he stayed overnight.

The fact that following this confrontation Knox could sleep
peacefully in a bed in Loch Leven Castle instead of being thrown
into a dungeon is a testimony to the strange truce which existed
between these two figures. One explanation is that Knox was
untouchable, protected by his former colleagues at court, and
useful to the English as an agitator. His arrest or execution would
have made Mary's position untenable. Compared with other
divided nations in Europe at this time the relationship between
the leading figures on the Protestant and Catholic sides in
Scotland was harmonious. There were no burnings, no
executions. A few demonstrations and some intimidation of
Catholics perhaps, but little of the violence which was a feature
of the French religious climate at the time. Mary might easily
have taken a decision to silence Knox, but she did not. Her
detractors − and that includes Knox in his written accounts
of these meetings − say that she was dissembling and all along
had a sinister motive in mind. More probably her tolerance had
behind it the hand of Lord James, who was present at the
meeting. He met Knox in his room afterwards, and then
persuaded the Queen to have another session with the preacher
the following day.

At dawn Knox received the summons to join the Queen out
in the country where she was hawking. He found her in relaxed
mood. She chatted in a friendly manner about a variety of topics,
and asked Knox's help with a marital problem between the Earl
of Argyll (a lord of the Congregation) and his wife, Mary's half-
sister, whom he was ill-treating. Knox warily agreed. She warned
him about scandal if one of the Huntly Gordons was made the
kirk's superintendent in Galloway (a warning Knox found to
be well-founded) and finally declared that she had thought it
over and would after all enforce the law about the mass. Knox
replied that if this were so she would have tranquillity in her

realm. Knox writes up the incident at length, he says, to show how duplicitous the Queen could be. But in this instance he plainly dissembled too, for when he wrote to Argyll about his marriage he added the advice that he should make sure he was in Edinburgh to sit on the bench at the trial of the Catholic prelates.

The Catholics were convicted and imprisoned, but the Queen had them released in May, which convinced Knox that the talk of enforcing the 1560 law had been hypocritical.

Two observations can be made about these confrontations with the Queen. The first is that they cannot have been as hate-ridden as Knox makes out. His *History* was written after the Queen's reputation had fallen into odium, when his own attitudes were spiced with venom. Secondly his own dealings with women usually brought out the charming side of him. The Holyrood meeting apart, the universally-recognised charm of Mary was bound to have had some effect and in their encounters it is not unlikely that there would have been some mutual respect and even humour. One can reasonably argue that there was chemistry between the two which attracted and repelled them at the same time. Knox and Mary were complete opposites, shadows of one another's personality. But when their mutual fascination became rejection, the rejection was all the more vehement. Mary and Knox were about to reach that explosive state.

Before we examine this, it is worth recording the gulf that had opened between Knox and the Protestant nobles with whom he had fought in 1559. In the spring of 1562 Knox had been asked to mediate in the feud between young Arran and Bothwell. The two came from rival dynasties and had fought on opposite sides in 1559, and both were arrogant and hot-blooded. Their feud had escalated when Bothwell and the Marquis d'Elboeuf both made a play for Arran's mistress in the winter of 1561–2. Bothwell, uncharacteristically, was repentant and told Knox he was planning to lead a more godly life. The preacher supervised a solemn hand-shaking at Hamilton House in Holy Week 1562. Then on Good Friday Arran burst into Knox's house, wildly claiming that Bothwell had asked him to join in a plot to kill Lord James and Lethington, kidnap the Queen, and take her to Dumbarton Castle where Arran would marry her. (Arran had shown signs of becoming infatuated with Mary despite gaining no favour at court.) The young nobleman manifested all the signs of paranoid schizophrenia and was put into confinement by his father, Chatelherault. However he escaped and blurted out his wild tale again to Lord James. Knox pointed out that the man was mad. But Lord James had already moved to arrest Arran and Bothwell, who were imprisoned in Edinburgh Castle. A few months afterwards Bothwell escaped abroad. Arran showed that Knox's assessment of his sanity had been correct. He subsequently accused his father of trying to kill him, and revealed his sexual delusions about the Queen. From them on he was confined. This bizarre footnote helps explain why Knox chose not to put his trust in princes. He was left feeling that both young madmen had made him look a fool.

Lord James and Lethington, on the other hand, were far from mad. They had temporarily given up the thought of marrying Mary into England and were helping her to further her dream of a marriage to Don Carlos of Spain. At first sight it seems that either they had lost their allegiance to protestantism or turned traitor. However their reasoning was that, since the Queen would have to ask permission of the nobles for such a marriage, they would make the religious settlement in favour of protestantism a condition of the union. It was a typical ploy of Lethington's and when Knox got to know about it through his excellent intelligence network, he set about putting a stop to it.

Parliament was about to go into session in June and the Queen opened it amid great pageantry and popularity. Knox growled from his pulpit about the 'stinking pride of women'. But he waited until the Parliament was fully in session and he had most of the nobility a captive audience at St Giles before he launched his most devastating attack:

I hear of the Queen's marriage: dukes, brethren to emperors, all strive for the best game. But this, my Lords, I will say – whensoever the nobility of Scotland professing the Lord Jesus, consents that an infidel (and all papists are infidels) shall be head to your sovereign, ye do so far as banish Christ Jesus from this realm; ye bring God's vengeance upon the country, a plague upon yourself, and perchance ye shall do small comfort to your sovereign.

This caused uproar, not simply among the Catholic nobility but among the Protestants, especially Lord James and Lethington, who had hoped to keep their delicate negotiations secret. Knox did not know that Don Carlos was mentally unstable but he had put his finger on the critical point at issue – the fate of the Reformation in Scotland depended on whether Mary married a Catholic or a Protestant.

Knox was summoned to Holyrood. Lord Ochiltrie and some of the Protestant lairds accompanied him but only Erskine of Dun was allowed to pass through the courtyard with him. Mary was shaking with emotion, whether from anger, frustration, hurt or anguish: all have been alleged. At the sight of Knox, she burst into tears. 'What have ye to do with my marriage?' she asked in a trembling voice. 'What are ye in this commonwealth?' (Knox then delivered the reply that ranks with Luther's famous 'Here I stand' speech.) Defiantly, he replied:

A subject born within the same, Madam. And albeit I be neither Earl, Lord nor Baron within it, yet has God made me (how abject I ever be in your eyes) a profitable member within the same. Yea, Madam, to me it appertains no less to warn of such things as may hurt it, if I foresee it, than it does to any of the nobility, for both my vocation and conscience crave plainness of me. And therefore, Madam, to yourself I say that which I speak in public place: whensoever that the Nobility of this realm shall consent that ye be subject to an unfaithful husband, they do as much as in them lieth to renounce Christ, to banish his truth from them, to betray the freedom of this Realm and perchance shall in the end do small comfort to yourself.

This reply reveals Knox's vision of the Scottish common man and an ideal of democracy, which would take another two centuries to win general acceptance. We can, in an age of religious tolerance, balk at the bigotry of Knox's language. But in 1563 the religious settlement could cut one of two ways, Protestant or Catholic. Knox had pronounced his prophecy and whatever else history may say of him, it cannot say that on this occasion he was mistaken.

The meeting ended with Knox expressing his sympathy and saying that he had no wish to see the Queen in tears. Mary spent an hour with Erskine before the two men left Holyrood together. Shortly after this interview Lord James was made Earl of Moray. Knox wrote him a somewhat brittle letter in which he offered his congratulations but added that in view of their differences he felt he could no longer be of use to him. It was a rift that was to last nearly two years.

The fifth and final time Knox stood in the presence of the Queen, he was on trial. The episode began later that year (1563) when Mary was away from Holyrood and mass was held there – in breach of the private agreement and of the law. Three Edinburgh burgesses burst in with pistols and broke up the service. Mary was furious at this insult to the palace territory and had the three summoned for trial on October 24. Knox issued a call for the Congregation throughout Scotland to attend Edinburgh on that date. But times had changed since the days when the Congregation could get their way by a manifestation of strength. This was viewed as sedition and Knox appeared before the Privy Council to answer for it. The occasion was charged with tension. All his old supporters, some of them now his critics, were there, as were his enemies. Knox's account (written after his stroke in 1571 and not considered totally reliable) portrays the Queen's behaviour as hostile and manic. He quotes her as saying in Scots (the tongue she would have known best after French): 'Yon man gart me greit, and grat never tear himself; I will see if I can gar him greit' (Now it's his turn to cry). Knox's defence was that he was simply carrying out the watchdog role committed to him by the General Assembly (which met a few days later and gave complete backing to his actions). At one point during his cross-examination by the Privy Council, Knox was called to order with the words, 'Ye forget yourself. Ye are not in the pulpit now!' But his performance must have been skilful, since, much to the Queen's frustration, the Privy Council did not find against him. Thus ended his final appearance before the Queen.

That dramatic episode in many ways symbolised what had happened to the Reform movement in three years. The Congregation, an unholy alliance of nobility and lower classes, had polarised. The Protestant lords were now sitting with the Queen and confronting the lower-class Protestants represented by Knox. The rift was complete and Knox was back where Wishart started. On his side he had many of the lairds and a section of the common people, but from that moment he was never able to influence political events on behalf of the Reformed Church. The new church itself was growing in numbers but was critically short of cash. Its General Assembly was emerging as a powerful voice, but it was a voice crying in a wilderness, a no man's land in which there was no settlement of religion. The Protestant nobles, such as Moray and Lethington, still attended the General Assembly but more as agents of the Queen's court than as Reformers, forcing its access to the monarch through their political filter. Knox's frustration was not entirely ill-founded.

The Hamiltons faded from the scene, and the return of the Catholic Earl of Lennox in September 1564 and the restoration of his lands signalled the beginning of a new era. There were concessions on both sides. On one hand the Privy Council saw to it that the kirk was supplied with some money and issued more decrees against the saying of mass. On the other hand the Archbishop of St Andrews resumed his seat in Parliament along with two of his colleagues. Knox thundered away in his pulpit, and if peace had not quite broken out on all sides, it seemed as if a kind of stability had been reached. It was not to last, for when Mary did finally find a husband, events were to take a more brutal and barbarous turn.

While all eyes were fixed on the marriage prospects of the Queen, John Knox caused a small sensation by getting married himself in the spring of 1564. He had been a widower for three years and his two small sons were being looked after by Mrs Bowes in Edinburgh. His new bride was Margaret Stewart, daughter of the Protestant Lord Ochiltrie and a descendant of the Royal Stewarts. She was seventeen and he was fifty. The

English ambassador Randolph reported to London that the Queen 'stormeth wonderfully' at the thought that she would now be distantly related to the preacher. He added that he was sorry about the marriage but does not say why. Knox's enemies indulged themselves liberally with innuendo about the couple's age difference and Catholic writers explained the match as having been brought about by witchcraft on Knox's part.

It is not hard to find a reason for Knox's wanting to marry again. Throughout his life he shows an inclination to give and receive emotional support from women, as we noted from the letters to Mrs Bowes and Mrs Locke. Nothing has survived to say why he chose Margaret Stewart but it is safe to assume that he met her through his visits to the Ochiltrie home in Ayrshire. There is no suggestion that her father disapproved or that it was an unhappy union. The charge of social climbing is difficult to bring against Knox, since he was in a much less influential position in 1564 with the nobility of Scotland. The explanation that Ochiltrie was an admirer of Knox's and that this hero-worship extended to his daughter is likely to be true.

There is a postscript to the event. After Knox married again, Mrs Bowes returned home to Northumberland, leaving behind the letters which have given so much insight into the private thoughts of Knox. There are no more Bowes letters during the coming years (nor to or from Anne Locke after 1562), and so we can only speculate whether a rift was caused by the second marriage, or whether the darker Knox who emerged in this period neglected his old friends. He certainly did not neglect his marital bed as Margaret bore him three daughters within two, four and six years of their wedding.

15

Gunpowder and Plots

Two Scottish monarchs have become internationally known through drama and opera. Both stories are tragedies and both involve dark forces. Macbeth, in the Shakespearean version if not in reality, precipitates his own destruction through ambition, and as the play progresses the atmosphere grows more malevolent. We have reached that point in the true story of the other tragic monarch, Mary Queen of Scots, when the darker forces come into play. From now on all the characters seem to be dominated by their least attractive aspects. It becomes a saga of the mad, the bad and the ugly.

We have already met two of the mad nobles, the schizoid Earl of Arran and the psychopathic Earl of Bothwell, the former locked away for the rest of his life and the latter pardoned and allowed back into Scotland. Into the tragedy at this point comes another unstable figure, eighteen-year-old Henry Stuart, Lord Darnley, son of the Earl of Lennox (who married the niece of Henry VIII after leaving for England twenty years previously). Lennox had a claim to the Scottish throne (see chart, p. 000), provided he could dispose of the Hamilton claimant (Chatelherault); and his son had a distant claim to the English throne. If Darnley married Mary it would greatly strengthen her ambition to be Queen of Scotland and England. Ironically it was Elizabeth who had given permission for Lennox and his son to return to Scotland in the spring of 1564, possibly a tactic to divert Mary from entering into the potentially-threatening alliance with Don Carlos of Spain. Knox lost no time in sending a letter to Sir William Cecil warning against the Catholic Darnley as a possible king; but by the time that Elizabeth woke up to the danger it was too late. Mary had fallen in love with the handsome earl when he was ill at Stirling in May 1564 and had nursed him personally. She had no eyes to see Darnley as the spoilt brat with the violent temper who emerged soon after their marriage on July 29 1565. She did not hear the warnings coming from Elizabeth that they would be enemies if the wedding went ahead. Mary was blind with love and deaf with ambition to be Queen of Britain. Darnley's goal was the crown matrimonial and he managed to convey the impression to both religious parties that he was sympathetic to their aims. He attended a service in St Giles, and avoided nuptial mass at his wedding. He was to be made king (without the crown matrimonial) and had almost achieved his aim. With Darnley asserting himself and assuming the title of King, Mary no longer needed the advice of Lord James Stewart, Earl of Moray, or of Maitland of Lethington, whose power base had been taken from under them.

Moray declared the marriage a disaster, since Scotland now had a Catholic monarchy. He began to organise a rebellion and succeeded in assembling a group which included Arran, Argyll and Glencairn, plus Kirkcaldy of Grange. The latter's military sense was always useful. Another member of the rebel band was Knox's father-in-law, Lord Ochiltrie. Several factors were against them. The machinations of Lord James had alienated him from the rank and file of the Congregation, on whom he could always count in the days when Knox was his close ally. The Queen herself had proved a popular monarch and when she announced that there was to be no change in the religious settlement, the people believed her. Moray was also to fail because the English Queen would not back him openly and only promised him asylum if he failed in his bid for power. His *coup d'état* was thus perceived as jealousy-inspired disaffection, a fusion of feudal hatred of the Lennoxes and religious opportunitism introduced for the sake of English subsidy.

Knox was well aware of these shortcomings in the rebels. His position in Edinburgh while the so-called Chaseabout Raid was in progress in the autumn of 1565 was extremely delicate. Darnley turned up at St Giles on August 19 to listen to Knox

preach and was given a throne-like chair on which to sit. Knox
spoke from the pulpit for an hour longer than usual and caused
Darnley to miss his dinner and be late for hawking. But that
was not the only thing that made the King angry. The serman
dealt with the sword of God, which Knox contended was not
intended for rulers to use as they pleased, but to punish vice:

> Kings then have not an absolute power in their regiment [rule]
> what pleaseth them; but this power is limited by God's word;
> so that if they strike where God commandeth not, they are
> murderers, and if they spare when God commandeth to strike,
> they and their throne are criminal and guilty of the wickedness
> that aboundeth upon the face of the earth for lack of
> punishment.

At every reference which might have borne upon his situation,
the people gawked across at Darnley, so that when Knox quoted
Isaiah 3:12: 'children are extortioners of my people and women
rule over them, 'there were no doubt a few pointed glances.
But when Knox dealt with Ahab, things got a little too close
for comfort:

> Did (Ahab) correct his idolatrous wife Jezebel? No – we find
> no such thing; but the one and the other we find to have
> continued and increased in former impiety. But what was the
> end thereof? The last visitation was that dogs licked the blood
> of the one and did eat the flesh of the other.

Darnley would have found Knox's sermons strong meat, but
to be preached at for such a long time while being gawked at
and subjected to such strong innuendo was too much to bear.
Knox was roused from his bed that night and required to appear
again before the Privy Council, who this time forbade him to
preach while the King and Queen were in Edinburgh. Although
the Burgh Council protested that it could never agree to have
Knox silenced in this way and requested that the order be
rescinded, Mary and Darnley had already marched out to
confront the rebels.

It is worth pausing to consider the astonishing position which

Knox held at this time. He had lost the protection of the leading lords, who were tired of him banging away at the revolutionary drum when they had made their own deal with the sovereign. Now these same lords had fallen out with the Queen, leaving Knox even more isolated. He had the Burgh Council of Edinburgh behind him, which was solidly Protestant, but the citizens were by no means unanimous in their affection for the new Calvinist religion. His English support was even more precariously based. The English ambassador and Cecil were happy to keep lines of communication open, but it was clear that they regarded Knox as having no locus in England and that if he became a liability to their own purposes, they would drop him at once.

Given the isolation of his position, and some of Knox's more extreme pronouncements, why did Mary not arrest him for heresy or treason? The reason why a heresy charge was not brought is not hard to find: with no religious settlement in Scotland the procedures for a heresy trial were in no man's land, since he could hardly have been asked to appear before Archbishop Hamilton. Nor was Knox's own church likely to have turned against him. However a charge of treason was a different matter. Initially Knox had been protected by the lords and used as their propagandist and verbal battering-ram. During the period 1560–4 he was still useful to them in his role as tribune of the people. The lords still needed the support of the Congregation until they could consolidate their position. Although they found Knox's revolutionary talk counter-productive (if not seditious), he was powerless except now and then to incite a few mobs to harass the Catholic population. They were prepared to reason with him (as they did at the meeting prior to the 1564 General Assembly), in order to keep his support. Once the lords rebelled against Mary, Knox would have been left extremely exposed, except for one thing. In order to prove that the lords were acting from their own base interests and not from religious principles, Mary had proclaimed 'no change' as far as religious toleration went, and she could hardly then move against the best-known name among the Protestant preachers. Knox was a thorn in the flesh of both sides but he was not lethal, and so he was tolerated.

As well as his acknowledged rhetorical skills, Knox won widespread respect because he had a genuine concern for those at the bottom of the social heap – provided they were godly in their outlook. His stipend at St Giles was originally £200, and then doubled to £400, making it high above the average minister's wage, but he fought hard to raise the stipends of his fellow-ministers, and for a greater share of the church taxes to go to the kirk, believing that only a properly-paid ministry could attract the right candidates.

After the harsh winters of 1563–4 and 1564–5 there was widespread starvation in Scotland. Appeals to the Queen in June and December 1565 to surrender her half of the third-share of the Old Church's benefices were refused (see p. 123). Knox wrote to the congregations explaining the poverty-stricken situation of many ministers and asking for voluntary contributions. Although we now take a system of voluntary contributions for granted, it was novel in the sixteenth century. Knox could have been making a stick with which to beat himself, since, if it was shown that the church could be funded by the middle classes, the nobles would cast off their obligations to maintain it through tithes. But the situation was desperate and Knox was willing to take the risk.

He outlined his thinking on the social obligations of the nobility and gentry at this time of widespread hardship, in *The Booke of the Universall Kirk* (December 28 1565). He said it was not enough to do unto others as they did to us, but the teaching of Christ was that we should do to others as we would wish them to do to us. He asked the nobles and gentry if they would be content if they were farm labourers and starved into leaving their homes and work ('for poverty the ancient labourers are compelled to leave the ground in the hands of the Lord'). Knox was not all bile and even in these embittered days there was still compassion for the common people from whom he came. One of the legacies of this period of privation for the Church of Scotland was that the ministers identified with the poverty of the people. This had a lasting effect on the character of Scotland's national church, which in subsequent centuries has more often leaned towards an institution of the people than of the ruling classes.

Meanwhile 1565 had ended with the ignominious flight of Lord James and his rebels into England after the Chaseabout Raid. Elizabeth, in a supreme example of perfidy, first repudiated the rebels and rebuked them for opposing their Queen, and then refused to hand them over to Mary. When the Scottish Queen discovered that the English ambassador Randolph had aided the rebels with money, she immediately expelled him.

The Queen of Scots was herself beginning to experience isolation. She had hoped to share the burdens of state with her new husband and consort, King Henry, whose head was on the coinage beside hers and whose signature was added to the foot of every royal proclamation. However Mary's kingly consort was a different man from the sickly lord who had composed love-poems to her in Stirling Castle. Now arrogant, quarrelsome, jealous and morally degenerate besides, Henry Darnley's true character had destroyed the Queen's happiness within a few months. But he had made her pregnant. Mary's baby would have equal claim to the thrones of England and Scotland, and this gave rise to tension and apprehension. Darnley's threatening behaviour towards his wife made many feel that he was psychotic. Mary had made him king because she believed she loved him. He in his turn thought the title was his by right. When Mary began to turn for advice in matters of state to her secretary, the Italian David Rizzio, Darnley was incensed. Rizzio did not make matters easier by the over-familiar way he behaved towards the Queen. Although most authorities are agreed that Rizzio was not her lover, despite the smears and innuendoes (in which Knox joined), there is no evidence to support the traditional accusations of nymphomania. (She had a young French poet executed after he intruded into her bedroom.)

The Protestant lords saw a way of using Darnley to recover a position of strength before the March Parliament, which was due to confiscate their lands. They signed a pact to kill Rizzio, of which Darnley was made the leader. This desperate deed was enacted on the night of March 9 in Holyrood Palace while the Queen was giving a dinner for friends in a small room leading from her suite. Darnley burst into the room together with Lord

Ruthven and other young bloods. They dragged the screaming Rizzio out and stabbed him to death.

The brutal slaying of Rizzio was hardly likely to have endeared Darnley to the Queen or enhanced his chances of gaining the crown matrimonial, the motive which has been put forward by some for his participation. Yet there might have been some method behind this madness. Andrew Ker of Faldonside put a pistol to the stomach of the pregnant Queen, and it has been plausibly argued that Darnley hoped the shock of the murder, and the pistol turned on her, would cause Mary to miscarry. In the mid-sixteenth century a miscarriage in the sixth month almost invariably meant the death of the mother; and Mary's death in these circumstances would have left Darnley King of Scots and claimant to the English throne.

Aware that something had happened within the Queen's apartments, the city alarms were sounded and crowds appeared around Holyrood. Darnley reassured them from a window that all was well and persuaded them to disperse. Those who had reason to fear for their own lives prepared to flee. The Earl of Bothwell, who was back in favour at court, escaped from the rear of Holyrood. The hated Friar John Black was not so lucky and was stabbed in his bed within the palace precincts. Now comes the twist in this tale of madness and murder. The Queen somehow persuaded Darnley to desert his conspirators and help her to flee. What she said or promised him is not recorded but, much as she must have feared and hated her husband, she prevailed upon him to escape with her to Dunbar Castle. Here they raised an army and on March 19 the Queen marched back in triumph to Edinburgh, a surly Darnley beside her. Mary's policy was now to do everything to guard the safety of her child and she moved her court into the impregnable fortress of Edinburgh Castle. Darnley skulked and sulked, his relations with the Queen even more sour than before. His fellow-conspirators had fled to England, from where Moray and his Chaseabout gang had now returned. They in turn were pardoned by Mary, who was desperate to preserve her life and that of her baby.

One of those alleged to have been privy to the plot was John Knox, who at this time went to Ayrshire. It would be naïve to think that Knox, with his close friendship with the lesser lairds in the Protestant party at court, would not at least have heard about the plot. In his *History* [Book I, 112] he sets down his hearty approval that the 'vile knave' Davy was 'justly punished . . . for abusing of the commonwealth and for his other villainy, which we list not to express'. No one alleged that Knox was an active participant in the killing; but was he in on the plot? A document discovered in the papers of Cecil has, written beneath a list of those known to be involved, the names 'John Knox, John Craig, preachers'. Cecil's clerk adds 'names of such as were consenting to the death of David'. If Knox had been shown to have been involved, even on the fringes of the conspiracy, he could not have avoided arrest. This could explain why he did not return to Edinburgh for five months, and even then it was briefly, to attend the General Assembly of December 1566: afterwards he slipped across the border into the north of England for another six months to visit his sons, finally returning to Edinburgh for the General Assembly of 1567. Was it guilt that caused him to stay away from the centre of events, fearful that he would be indicted as a conspirator? It is also possible that Knox was waiting to see how events would turn out. He was unable to influence the power struggle within the court and preferred to play a waiting game at a distance.

Those who wish Knox to end his days unsullied by conspiracy would want us to believe that the year he was away from his pulpit was devoted to writing further parts of the *History of the Reformation*. Factually this is true, but when we examine what he wrote in Book I we see a different John Knox from the man who worked for a solution to the troubles at Frankfurt. There is spite and hatred in this writing. Mary Queen of Scots is a whore and a Jezebel. Her mother, Mary of Guise, is worse, and there is even a slur that her daughter is illegitimate, without evidence being offered. He gloats and revels in the downfall of Mary of Guise in an embarrassing way and indulges himself in little asides about hated characters (for example he calls one man who is the illegitimate son of a priest 'gett' [bastard]). He rejoiced that Mary's first husband King Francis had died from a mastoid infection in his ear, 'that deaf ear that would never hear the Word of God'.

His former ally Lord James, not yet restored to favour, also comes in for criticism. Pessimism, gloom and rancour hang like a cloud over these pages. In this book Knox proves to be his own worst enemy and tarnishes the reputation which he had fought hard to establish. There is a Scots word, 'thrawn', which means wilfully difficult, grumbling and uncooperative. Knox was certainly that during this long vacation; he even turned on the Non-conformists in England, who came to him in admiration, asking for backing in their quarrel with Grindal, Bishop of London. He told them they had no right to form a breakaway church and they should conform. This was a profound change of opinion for the man who was once a rebel in Cranmer's church.

The young prince James was born in July 1566. The Queen's careful handling of Darnley had paid off, for a divorce or a public separation around the time of the birth would have attracted debate about the child's legitimacy. At the time there were gibes about 'Davy's bairn', despite the fact that Mary's friendship with Rizzio grew strong only after she was pregnant; and Rizzio was by some accounts a physically ugly specimen. Prince James was baptised a Catholic and this fuelled Knox's fears about the future. The birth of an heir to the throne also reduced Darnley's chances of the succession and he began behaving in his previously psychotic way, spending little time with the Queen. There were whispers that he was again plotting against his wife.

Mary's counsellors now included two 'Protestants' – Bothwell and Maitland of Lethington, who had been re-admitted to her favour in September. These two, and fellow-conspirator Lord Morton, began to hatch a plot to remove the dangerous and paranoid Darnley. There have been many accounts of the episode which led to the assassination of the King, and many explanations of who was involved and why.

One version is that the intention was to kill the King and Queen with the one explosion. It is certainly true that Darnley was ill early in 1567 with the 'pox'. Examination of his bones has shown that he almost certainly had syphilis. He was persuaded to return to Edinburgh for convalescence, since any plot against his life would have had less chance of succeeding in the Lennox Stewart stronghold in the west of Scotland. He stayed at the Balfour mansion in Kirk o'Field, just outside the walls of Edinburgh, less than a mile from Holyrood. The house faced across the quadrangle to the town house of his rivals the Hamiltons. Mary paid him regular visits and stayed in the room beneath his. She may or may not have known what was being planned but was conveniently back at Holyrood at a celebration for the wedding of one of her ladies-in-waiting on February 9 1567 when the explosion happened. This gunpowder plot, like another more famous one half a century later, was only partly successful. The house was blown up but Darnley had been warned, or else had spotted the men from the Douglas and Hepburn clans whom the Earl of Bothwell had assembled. The twenty-one-year-old King fled in his nightgown across the garden with a servant. As dawn broke, their strangled bodies were found.

The behaviour of the Queen at this point has been interpreted variously. The stresses and strains of the past few years had undoubtedly affected her health and composure. She apparently saw the murder as aimed also at her. In a state of shock and in need of a strong protector, she turned to Bothwell. That is one theory and there are several others which involve the Queen in various degrees of stupidity and cupidity. But all the historians agree that Bothwell was responsible for the death of Darnley and that Mary's behaviour in the period following the Kirk o'Field murder was not that of a grief-stricken widow. The public at the time thought Bothwell guilty. Placards appeared in Edinburgh with the Queen portrayed suggestively as a mermaid and Bothwell as a hare (his family crest). By the end of March Drury, the English ambassador, reported that the judgment of the people was that Bothwell and the Queen would marry. Lennox brought a private prosecution against Bothwell for the murder of his son, and the swashbuckling earl responded by marching an army into Edinburgh on the day of his trial and challenging his accusers to combat. There was more than a little of the buccaneer about Bothwell. His intimidation worked to the extent that Lennox failed to make an appearance and Bothwell was declared innocent.

By April 19 Bothwell was sufficiently confident to invite a group of nobles and lairds to Ainslie's Tavern for a lavish dinner.

Rather in the style of a mafia boss, he produced a paper for them to sign which not only declared him innocent but went on to state that since the Queen was now 'destitute of a husband, in which solitary state the commonwealth will not permit her to remain', it would be fitting if she would agree to choose 'the affectionate and hearty service of the said Earl' for her husband, since he was a native-born subject and not a foreigner. Eight bishops, nine earls and seven barons put their signatures to this, including the Lords Morton, Maitland, Argyll, Huntly (son of the rebel, see p. 136) and Glencairn. The fact that Bothwell was still married to his wife Jean did not seem to have influenced this gathering of unscrupulous and desperate men one jot. Such was the condition of the Scottish nobility in the second half of the sixteenth century that double-crosses, murder and a press-gang marriage for their sovereign were considered legitimate courses of action. Religion was but one convenient excuse for what had become the raw pursuit of personal advantage. One can have sympathy for Knox's despair when he saw his godly revolution gone to seed in this way, if not for his failure to condemn its hypocrisy as he had condemned the old regime.

Knox was still in England, as was Moray (Lord James) when these events happened. The Queen decided to visit her baby son at Stirling Castle, the safe haven she had previously enjoyed in her own infancy. She wrote from there to the former papal nuncio, who was now in Turin, protesting her devotion to Scotland and the Catholic Church, and declaring that she had every intention of dying a Roman Catholic. On April 22 1567 she started back for Edinburgh, staying *en route* at Linlithgow Palace where she was born. The next morning as she set out for the capital, Bothwell appeared with a force of 800 men, and catching hold of her bridle explained that as there was danger threatening her in Edinburgh, he was taking her to Dunbar.

Following the route which is now Edinburgh's southern by-pass motorway, they arrived at his castle in East Lothian, where Bothwell forced his suit. Ravishment, rape, entrapment, were all words used for what happened. Suffice it to say that within three weeks they were married. Knox's colleague John Craig refused to read the wedding banns until he had the Queen's assurance that she had not been ravished. He was sent it in writing, along with a threat from Bothwell to hang him. Bothwell got his divorce on May 3 in the Protestant court and for good measure the Roman Catholic Archbishop Hamilton annulled his marriage on May 7. On May 12 he became Duke of Orkney and the couple were married in a Protestant ceremony on May 15 with only a meagre feast to follow. The papacy washed its hands of Mary, and the nobility began to fall out among themselves. The thuggish Bothwell behaved like the epitome of male chauvinism towards his Queen. Maitland poisoned the Queen's ears with the word that Bothwell was still intimate with his ex-wife and the atmosphere grew more like that of the final act of *Macbeth*.

The nobles now began to group against Bothwell. At the beginning of June, after a month of marriage, the Queen and Bothwell were opposed by an army of rebels led by many of the men who had signed the Ainslie bond. To add yet another twist of treachery, the man who sent word to the Queen that her position would be stronger if she moved from East Lothian (a Bothwell stronghold) back to Edinburgh was one Sir James Balfour, who had shared an oar with Knox in the galleys. It was Balfour who had betrayed Darnley in his family home at Kirk o'Field and he was now, in exchange for a pardon and preferment, entrapping the Queen. When they reached Carberry Hill behind Musselburgh, not two miles from the bloodstained soil of Pinkie Cleugh, the two forces met on Sunday, June 15 1567. The nobles called on Mary to renounce Bothwell, promising that they would once again pledge allegiance to her. Recognising that those facing her were mostly the signatories of the bond which had encouraged her to wed Bothwell in the first place, she refused. The battle was quickly over. Bothwell fled to Orkney and subsequent exile, and the Queen was led through ranks of jeering troops who called for her death. She was imprisoned in Loch Leven Castle, where she used to go hawking. The man she had once confronted there swooped back to his pulpit in Edinburgh, like a hawk coming in for the kill.

16

Unquiet Spirit

Knox was not gracious to the Queen in her downfall. He called for her death, not once but in every single sermon. Elizabeth of England was affronted that monarchy could be treated in this way but her advisers Throckmorton and Cecil were careful to remind her that if the English Queen moved to help her Scottish cousin, the Scots were ready to renew their old alliance with France. Moray had already visited the French court and du Croc, the French ambassador, conveyed the message that the King of France would be prepared to deal with the lords and leave Mary out of it. Knox was thundering in his pulpit against the idea of a French alliance and exhorting an English – Scottish alliance of Protestant nations, unaware that Elizabeth was leaning to Mary, and threatening to invade Scotland if its sovereign was put to death. On July 24 the lords forced Mary to abdicate in favour of her infant son, who was crowned James VI in the church of the Holy Rood, Stirling, on July 29. Knox preached at the coronation and, along with the Justice Clerk and a Protestant laird, was selected to 'ask instruments', a legal gesture which recognised the quasi-established role of the Protestant religion in the new King's realm. He significantly refused to participate in anointing the King as part of the ceremony.

The postponed Reformation now took place: the Scots Parliament of December 1567 endorsed all that had been done in 1561 including the ratification of the Scots Confession drafted by the preachers. Future kings were to swear at their coronation that they would govern by the Word of God revealed in the Old

and New Testaments. All officers of state were to profess the
Reformed religion and all teachers in school were under approval
of the church. The kirk was to have a full third of the old
benefices. And church courts were able to punish moral offences
such as fornication. It was not quite the Book of Discipline as
they wrote it, but it would have to do. This was Reformation in
the style of Lord James Stewart, Earl of Moray, rather than the
style of Knox.

The mood in the country had changed and there was less joy
in the vision. The church courts began to enforce the new religion
with a dogged persistence. Mary was officially indicted (without
benefit of defending herself) of complicity in the murder of
Darnley on the basis of the 'Casket letters', although their
authenticity is doubted by her supporters. If proof is also needed
that the Reformation which had taken place did not bring deep
satisfaction to those who led it, it rests in their actions. John
Willock went to England, and Knox was asked by the Assembly
to order him back to his parish in January 1568. Willock complied
but left soon afterwards to end his days as Rector of
Loughborough. Another close colleague of Knox's also opted
for England: Christopher Goodman had departed in 1565 to
become a vicar.

What of Knox himself? Throughout his life his thoughts had
often turned to England, and now was no exception. His sons
were being educated there, and on February 14 1568 he wrote
to his friend John Wood, who had been sent by the Regent on
a mission to England:

> God comfort that dispersed little flock amongst whom I once
> lived with quietness of conscience and contentment of heart;
> and amongst whom I would be content to end my days, if so
> might stand with God's good pleasure . . . I would even as
> gladly return to them, if they stood in need of my labours, as
> ever I was glad to be delivered from the rage of mine enemies.
> I can give you no reason that I should desire, other than my
> heart so thirsteth.

Knox's lack of ease in Scotland was further undermined by
the escape of the Queen from Loch Leven Castle on May 2 1568.

She took refuge with the Hamiltons and was soon joined by nine earls, eighteen lords and nine bishops. These 'Queen's lords' issued a proclamation offering to pardon any of the rebels who submitted, but castigated some of the nineteen leading nobles with an invective that would have done Knox proud. Although the list goes from Morton ('beastly traitor') and Mary's half-brother Lord James Stewart, Earl of Moray ('bastard gotten in shameful adultery') to 'hellhounds' like Andrew Ker, the list of 'godless traitors' does not include any reference to Knox himself. 'Mischievous ministers whose sermons seduce the people' are mentioned, but no names. Now allied with Chatelherault and the Hamiltons, the Queen needed to win the support of Scottish Protestants and she was not going to make religion an issue in this struggle for power.

The crucial battle took place at Langside, on the south side of Glasgow, on May 17 1568. Although the Queen's forces outnumbered the 'King's lords', the military skills of Lord James, Morton and Kirkcaldy of Grange helped the latter's army win the day. Mary fled into England and asked for help to restore her throne. Elizabeth stalled. She was waiting until Mary was proved innocent of Darnley's murder, and probably to protect her interests which would prosper better with Lord James holding the reins of power in Scotland. In August 1568 the Queen's lords assembled in the north and west, and were poised to attack again when Elizabeth persuaded them to sue for a truce. Mary agreed and in doing so lost the advantage which lay with her at that moment. She was never to regain it.

The English Queen now held the key to the Scottish situation. She had Mary in her power but though she continued to favour the 'King's men', in the minds of the Scots Protestant leaders there must have been a lingering suspicion that she might still settle with Mary and plunge Scotland back into turmoil. Against this background English Catholics in the north-east of England rebelled against Elizabeth, but were quickly crushed. Elizabeth could now see that Mary posed a danger to her and thus continued her policy of comfortable confinement for her cousin.

In 1569 plans were afoot for Mary Queen of Scots to marry the Duke of Norfolk. These were entertained by the King's lords in Scotland up to July of that year, when they eventually voted at Perth 40 to 9 against the Queen's return. Elizabeth's policy of suspicious toleration towards her reluctant detainee lasted through the Ridolfi plot (in which a Spanish adventurer was to kill Elizabeth and put Norfolk and Mary on the English throne). Eventually the Scottish Queen made her last mistake by involving herself in the Babington plot against her cousin Elizabeth, and was beheaded in 1586.

Knox did not live to see her end, but had called for it often enough. After the rising of 1570 he wrote to Cecil on January 2, 'If ye strike not at the roots, the branches that appear to be broken will bud again with greater force than we would wish', echoing his earlier reputed remark when the monasteries were being sacked that 'crows' nests should be knocked down so that the crows cannot nest in them again'. He signed this letter 'John Knox with one foot in the grave'.

Death was to come to Moray sooner. On January 21 1570 as he rode through Linlithgow the Regent was shot from the window of the house of John Hamilton, Archbishop of St Andrews. The assassin was the prelate's nephew, who escaped to France and was later rewarded by Mary. Knox had been reconciled with Moray and he preached that Sunday in praise of the Regent, whose only failing, he declared, had been that he spared the life of 'that most wicked woman'. At the funeral Ochiltrie was one of the pall-bearers, Kirkcaldy of Grange walked in front of the coffin with Moray's banner, and Knox preached on the text 'Blessed are the dead which die in the Lord' (Rev.14:13), to a tearful congregation. The haunting folk song, 'The bonny Earl o'Moray', keeps alive to this day the memory of the best 'king' that Scotland never had.

Moray's death sparked off another civil war with the Hamiltons, who became the focus of the hatred of the King's lords. They fought back successfully and at one point the Queen's lords looked like triumphing, until Elizabeth sent in an English army under the Earl of Sussex, which crushed them. The Earl of Lennox, despite being a Catholic and an English citizen, was installed as Regent of a Protestant nation. The Queen of Scots still had some support in the north, and Edinburgh Castle was held by Kirkcaldy of Grange, who had been persuaded by Lethington to defect to the Queen's side and to release

Chatelherault from his custody. This betrayal by one of the early Protestants was a bitter pill for Knox. He criticised Kirkcaldy in sermons and the latter responded with threats against Knox. The strain on Knox was telling and in the autumn of 1570 he suffered a stroke, which was interpreted by his enemies as divine retribution. But he had not lost his fight and was back in action in the pulpit within months.

The decade 1560–70 was unstable, violent and unpredictable. Some of the leading nobles changed sides several times and could in no way be described by the simple label either of Catholic or Protestant. This was not a religious war, or even a civil war, so much as a mafia feud. Knox remained true to his ideology but even he was compromised by the shifting sands of loyalties and political fortunes. He supported the plea of the General Assembly in June 1570 that all ministers should pray for the King on pain of excommunication, but there were still supporters of the Queen within the kirk who wanted to pray for her conversion. A growing faction wanted to keep out of this bitter conflict and remain neutral between the King's and Queen's men, but in Knox's eyes this was to be neutral between Protestant and Catholic, God and the devil. His forthright sermons, despite failing health, continued to hammer this home and inevitably in the divided city he attracted hatred.

Lethington's younger brother Thomas, who had hated Moray, circulated a satire in the form of a conversation between Knox and Moray in which the preacher urged the Regent to kill King James, announcing that he was preparing a Second Blast in which he would prove that bastards could inherit the crown. One of Knox's supporters read this and asked him if it was true. Knox denounced the author from the pulpit. Thomas Maitland was also the author of a note left in Knox's pulpit the Sunday after Moray's assassination, which said, 'Take up the man whom you accounted another God, and consider the end whereto his ambition hath brought him'. Knox was not the kind of man to ignore such a challenge and reputedly prophesied that the author would not go unpunished 'and shall die where none shall be to lament him'. Lethington died at the age of twenty-two while travelling in Italy; and this, along with other prophesies of Knox's (for example that he would return to preach in St Andrews and

St Giles), contributed to his legend as a 'prophet', begun by
Smeton within a few years of Knox's death and enlarged by
Thomas McCrie's influential biography in the early nineteenth
century.

A few hundred yards up the road from St Giles sat Kirkcaldy
of Grange and Lethington, holding the castle for the Queen.
Some of their soldiers saw fit to name a cannon 'Knox'. Soon
afterwards it exploded, killing some of the battery, and this too
was seen as prophetic. Knox never mended the breach with
Kirkcaldy, who had been through two decades of struggle with
him. (One report of a visit to the castle by a 'master John' and
a friendly dialogue while Lethington played with a little dog has
been convincingly shown [Ridley, p. 548] not to refer to Knox.
One might add that since nearly all the prominent Protestant
ministers in this period seem to have been called John, there were
a lot of possible candidates.) The question why Grange and
Lethington did not march down the Royal Mile and arrest Knox
is easily answered. The Queen's party made much of the fact that
the King's party was led by the Catholic Lennox. They did not
want to be portrayed as the Catholic party and they could not
silence the kirk's most prominent preacher. But there were others
who tried. Knox had moved into a larger house in Trunk Close
on his return to Edinburgh in 1567 and used to sit in a chair with
its back to the window. One night a shot passed through the chair
and hit the chandelier, missing Knox who on this occasion was
sitting at the side of the table.

Assassination by commando raids was becoming more
common. Dumbarton Castle was recaptured by the King's men
and Archbishop Hamilton was taken prisoner and hanged. In
retaliation the Queen's men marched on Edinburgh and
Kirkcaldy ordered all Lennox's supporters to leave town. Knox
at first refused but was persuaded to go to St Andrews, where
his nephew Paul had gone to study. (This was his brother
William's son, who had stayed at Trunk Close with him in 1567.)
In July 1571 Knox took a boat across to Fife. No sooner was he
out of Edinburgh than Kirkcaldy's soldiers assembled cannon
on the roof of St Giles, from where they bombarded Morton's
soldiers in their trenches in the Canongate, causing havoc in the
heart of the capital. The Protestant Bishop of Galloway occupied

Knox's pulpit and preached sermons which acknowledged that although Mary had sinned she was as lawful a Queen as David was King of Israel after he had committed adultery. Kirkcaldy struck a blow for his side by sending a commando force of 400 to Stirling where they managed to capture and kill the Regent Lennox.

Away from these provocations in St Andrews, Knox might have enjoyed peace and the chance to recuperate, but controversy followed him there. The bitter conflict in Scottish life over the monarchy had divided the town and the university. Two colleges, St Mary's and St Salvator's, were sympathetic to the Queen's party, but Knox found solace and support in St Leonard's and lodged with Winram in the old priory. He used to sit in the college yard, and the diary of James Melville describes him as acting like an elder statesman towards the young students. He no doubt appreciated a satirical play which they put on, which ended with the Castilians of Edinburgh being hanged. Melville also records that Knox preached daily, although he walked with a stick and had to be helped into the pulpit by his servant Bannatyne, whose diary also provides glimpses of Knox's twilight years. On one occasion he began to preach, and reaching the inevitable denunciations of Mary, the Hamiltons or Kirkcaldy he became so violent in thumping the pulpit that Melville could scarcely concentrate on holding his pen, but managed to describe in a memorable Scots phrase this tub-thumping oratory as 'dinging the blads'. On another occasion while Knox preached a convicted witch was chained to a pillar facing the pulpit. Knox denounced witchcraft and after the service she was executed.

But it was his statement that 'Hamiltons are murderers', and the vivid prophecies that Edinburgh Castle would burst like a sandglass and spew Kirkcaldy over the wall, which upset Goodman's successor as parish minister, Robert Hamilton, then a leading figure in St Mary's College. When it reached Knox's ears that Hamilton had said Knox was as great a murderer as any Hamilton because he had once plotted with Moray to murder Darnley, Knox threatened to sue for slander and Hamilton was quick to deny he had ever said it.

A more important contentious issue landed on Knox's doorstep in St Andrews. Since the hanging of Archbishop Hamilton the archbishopric and primacy lay vacant. Despite the fact that Scotland did not acknowledge the jurisdiction of the pope, it did recognise a legal right to the benefice, and the right of the holder to sit in Parliament. The Earl of Mar had become Regent after the death of Moray and together with the Privy Council had reached an agreement with the kirk in January 1572 that, on condition that they appointed Protestant ministers, the nobles could have the income from these bishoprics. The bishops thus appointed were known as 'tulchan bishops', derived from the practice of putting a stuffed calfskin (or tulchan) underneath a cow in order to induce it to give milk. Lord Morton was given the right of appointment to St Andrews and appointed John Douglas Rector of St Andrews University. Knox was asked to install Douglas and refused, despite his bond with him. Such a fraudulent system went against all that he had fought for. He preached at the service but made no reference whatsoever to its purpose, and then Winram stepped forward and installed his colleague Douglas as Rector. Knox did not go as far as to attack Morton for his avarice or denounce the system, but it is hardly surprising that he did not approve of such procedures.

In view of the subsequent imposition of bishops upon the Church of Scotland by James I, and by both Charles I and Charles II, and the perennial bitterness the issue had caused within the kirk, it is worth considering what Knox's attitude was to bishops in principle. He clearly did not regard them as unscriptural during his time in England, but the thrust of his ecclesiology and the First Book of Discipline do not favour an episcopal form of church government. In short, he was not fundamentally opposed to bishops but was happy to live without them. This 'moderate' position conflicts with some of the positions attributed to him posthumously, but accords with the facts.

A further unpleasant incident occurred during July, Knox's last month in St Andrews. A student called Archibald Hamilton had refused to attend Knox's services because of his accusation that the Hamiltons were murderers. The student appealed to Archbishop Douglas, who visited Knox but was firmly told by the preacher that the church must be preserved from the 'bondage of the universities'. It is clear that Knox regarded Douglas as having no locus as Archbishop but only as Rector of the university. Knox contented himself with the knowledge that the General Assembly was about to clip Douglas's wings by ruling on whether or not it was proper for a bishop of a large diocese at the same time to be Rector of a university.

But larger problems loomed. The Ridolfi plot to put Mary Queen of Scots on the English throne was in full swing and there was a possibility that Fernando of Toledo, Duke of Alva would land an army to link up with Edinburgh Castle and restore Mary to the Scottish throne. Knox's letter on July 19 1572 to Wishart of Pitarrow is a pessimistic and heartfelt expression of his weariness with the way things had turned out:

Both the parties stand fighting against God himself in justification of their wickedness; the murderers assembled in the castle of Edinburgh and their assisters, justifying all that they have done to be well and rightly done; and the contrary party as little respecting the troubling and oppressing of the poor Church of God as ever they did. For if they can have the Church lands to be annexed to their houses, they appear to take no more care of the instruction of the ignorant and the feeding of the flock of Jesus Christ than ever did the papists, whom we have condemned, and yet are worse ourselves in that behalf.

This reveals that Knox the idealist had not died, and although he was too weary and too cynical and too pragmatic by now to say so in public, he saw with clarity what had happened. By now he was convinced his end was near. He was spending most of the time in bed and wrote to Goodman that they had no hope of meeting again in this life.

On July 31 the King's and Queen's parties agreed to a truce under pressure from France and England, who were fearful of Spanish intervention. Although Kirkcaldy of Grange and Maitland of Lethington remained in control of the castle, Edinburgh was now at peace again and Knox was asked to return. Some of the Congregation were not happy with the neutral attitude which John Craig had been adopting in his sermons. When Knox returned he was so weak that his voice could not be heard and it was arranged for him to have a small part of the Tolbooth church in which he could preach. This was situated just across the Royal Mile from the lodgings at Trunk's Close, a splendid house owned by James Mossman the goldsmith, confiscated when he became one of the Queen's party in the castle, and open to the public today as 'John Knox House' with its museum.

It was here Knox came to die, within sight of St Giles and the castle, the two landmarks of Edinburgh's skyline which could still rouse his emotions. His last letters concern them both. He promoted as his successor at St Giles James Lawson of Aberdeen University, who was invited to come to preach. 'Make haste, my brother,' wrote Knox on September 7, 'lest you come too late.' But Knox lived to see Lawson inducted as his successor on November 9. Then after saying a few words from the pulpit, which no one could discern, the stooped figure with the long beard walked slowly down the Royal Mile, leaning on his stick and followed by his congregation, a Moses in the wilderness.

Despite his failing health, Knox was well enough to receive the new English ambassador, Killigrew, who had been commissioned to find out whether the King's lords were interested in putting Mary on trial in Scotland. We may be sure what Knox replied if his opinion was canvassed on that prospect. He also took the opportunity to warn the ambassador against Kirkcaldy of Grange and Maitland of Lethington. The enmity was mutual, as Lethington had complained that very week to the Kirk Session that Knox had called him an atheist. When the session brought him this news, Knox riposted that, although he had not used these words, the godlessness of Lethington was amply demonstrated by the ruined houses demolished by the castle's cannon. Knox also received a visit on his death-bed from Lord Morton, who had taken over as Regent after the death of Mar through illness. Morton was subsequently executed for his involvement in the murder of Darnley. His confession of June 15 1581 reveals that he lied to Knox during this visit, when he denied involvement in the Darnley plot [Bannatyne].

Knox had ordered his coffin during his last week of life. He also ordered a new hogshead of wine to be opened and urged his guests to drink freely since he would not live to finish it. (There is some irony in this gesture since some modern Calvinists would prefer to think that Knox was a teetotaller, whereas he shared the habits of his epoch in which ale or claret was the standard accompaniment to food.) On his final day, November 24, he managed to get up and dress and asked his wife to read chapter 15 of I Corinthians, which deals with death. As she read, he commended himself to God, soul, body and spirit, ticking them off on his fingers as he spoke. At 5 p.m. he told his wife, 'Go read where I first cast my anchor' (John 18), the story of Gethsemane. Then as prayers were said over him in his bed at ten o'clock the physician asked if he could hear. Knox replied, 'I would to God that ye and all men heard them as I have heard them; and I praise God of that heavenly sound.' At eleven o'clock John Knox, wielder of the sword of the Lord, at last gained his peace.

Knox was buried in the churchyard adjoining St Giles, which today is a car park for the Court of Session. A small plaque on car space no. 44 marks the spot. For centuries his immense contribution to Scottish history had no tangible memorial, until a statue was erected this century in the small quadrangle between the General Assembly hall and New College, Edinburgh, in which the preacher stands, remonstrating finger held aloft. It was in this dismal courtyard in 1982 that the Pope met the Moderator of the General Assembly, but no cameras were permitted in that part of the courtyard, which would have resulted in a photograph in which the wagging finger hovered disapprovingly over the two men. Knox, at that moment, was an embarrassment to his church, as he had often been during his lifetime. Yet without him it is doubtful if it would have existed in anything like the form it does today.

His personal legacy to his family was £1,526, a sizeable sum at the time, of which over half was owed to him in debts (including £80 owed by his father-in-law Lord Ochiltrie). He left £500 to Robert Bowes, Marjory's brother, in trust for his two sons, both of whom went to Cambridge University: Eleazer died through illness, aged twenty-three, and Nathaniel became Vicar of Clacton but died in 1591 aged thirty-two. His nephew Paul Knox was left £100 towards his education; and the rest went to his wife Margaret and her three daughters. Margaret Knox married Andrew Ker of Faldonside (one of Rizzio's killers) within two years and their son became a kirk minister. Two of Knox's daughters by Marjory Bowes also married ministers.

Knox's legacy to Scotland was immense but it is sometimes distorted. A common myth is that he was the founder of presbyterianism. That title rightly belongs to Andrew Melville who rose to influence in the years following Knox's death and produced the Second Book of Discipline in 1581, which laid the foundations of the Presbyterian system which Scotland's national church still has today. Between the victory of 1560 and Knox's death in 1572 the alliance between church and state in Scotland had evolved through several stages. Initially there was a period when the Roman Catholic Church ceased to have any legal recognition as a church but was allowed to exist as a legal entity within the Three Estates of Parliament. The legal right to raise money from benefices was preserved but the Catholic Church was prevented access to this. The official position of the state on matters of belief was the Scots Confession (co-authored by Knox) but it is noteworthy that this document was not put forward by the church or imposed by the state, which simply 'ratified and approved (it) as wholesome and sound doctrine'. The Confession was treated not so much as a constitution as a statement of truth. It was not until 1567 that the Church of Scotland was given legal definition as an institution of the realm, when the people who professed their faith in the 'reformit kirkis' were defined 'to be the only trew and haly kirk of Jesus Christ within this realme' [Church Act 1567, c.6, re-enacted 1579, c.6].

The Church Jurisdiction Act 1567, clause 12 took a further step when it declared and granted jurisdiction to the Reformed Church: 'Thair is na uther face of Kirk nor uther face of religion than is presentlie be the favour of God establischeit within this realme and that thair be na uther iurisdiction ecclesiasticall acknawlegeit . . .' However the problem was that this did not make clear whether the state recognised the jurisdiction that the kirk had been exercising since 1560; or whether the declaration involved additional powers being conferred by the state. This may seem an abstruse point, since it quite clearly establishes the kirk as the sole and supreme church, but it was to cause problems in later centuries in deciding the question.

When the Concordat of Leith in 1572 redistributed the benefices of the Old Church, it also produced legislation which allowed the state to depose ministers who did not subscribe to the Scots Confession. The total effect of the Acts of 1567 and 1572 was to convert the benefices for the use of the church, but nothing was done to recover the benefices which had passed to secular control or the wealth of monasteries and abbeys which had not been taken over by the kirk. In other words the net effect was to make it possible for the Crown to claim that the kirk was under its control, whereas the vision of Knox was of a church free from state control and independent in its powers. Knox's failure to win this point in the early years resulted in two major confrontations on the question of church – state relations. In the seventeenth century the Covenanters fought to establish that independence and in the nineteenth century it led to the Disruption when a large section of the kirk seceded from the established church over the issue of state control. Both groups claimed allegiance to Knox's vision and they were right to do so. But they were on less sure ground in claiming that Knox had established such a free and independent kirk. It was his failure to do so that was the major source of his frustration and bitterness in his later years.

Andrew Melville stepped into the shoes of Knox and became the scourge of James VI (and I), as Knox had been of Mary. But James went further than his mother in two respects. His 'Black Acts' of 1584 asserted Crown control over the church. He united the realms of Scotland and England under his kingship in 1603 and this made it possible for his son Charles I to try to absorb the Scottish Church into the English structure of church and state. Thus the tensions which Knox had found between the English model (church as a function of the apparatus of state) and the Scottish model (church as counterbalance to state) surfaced again. So too did the question whether the sovereign's God-given rights could be modified or withdrawn. Although subsequently much of the debate in Scotland focused around bishops (who were the vanguard of the King's policy of subjugation), Knox had already anticipated this threat to his vision. He had provided a tradition and a critique which enabled the Scottish Church to attack the pretensions of the kings and preserve the independence of their religion from state control. He handed on his sword to the next generation.

17

The Sword and the Spirit

Any biographer of John Knox is presented with a succession of *personae*. First the Lothian lad who became a priest and was tutor to a laird's family near his home. Next the thirty-year-old who discovered the new religion being spread by the European Protestants, and along with it his own talents as a preacher. Then the man of steel who was tempered in the flames of conflict; followed by the visionary of the Book of Discipline. Finally, in his last years, the angry man whose judgments were often warped by his disappointments. We can be forgiven for asking if the real John Knox will please stand up.

Many of these *personae* came about as his response to situations. In general, Knox did not control the events in his life: he was called, sent, imprisoned, commanded, invited, elected and denied. That was partly because his was a world in which the destinies of people's lives were decided by kings and nobility, or by the princes of the church. Knox was born and remained an underling in that world. He did not have power to command, dispose or assign, apart from exercising his freedom to refuse the two appointments offered to him in England. He remained dependent for the achievement of his aims upon others who did possess that power. Realising that, he worked pragmatically within the rules of the game, playing the role for which he was best suited – that of a persuader.

It is when he gets into the pulpit that he is liberated from the constraints of the princes. Here he is truly free to promote what he sees as truth and to exhort, condemn and judge. To assess Knox fully we must therefore look at what he identified as truth and, although we have seen a man of action rather than a thinker who derived his actions from his ideology, the core of Knox's beliefs are essential to understanding him and the times in which he lived.

Although the battle of ideas in the sixteenth century was considered to be between truth and falsity, right religion and heresy, we are less willing to take sides with such absolute certainty. We are more relative in our thinking than Knox could ever have been. Thus we do not say simplistically, 'Knox said or did that because he had the truth and the others were wrong'. We can easily concede that if we had to choose between the corrupt church in which Knox was brought up and the one he wanted, the latter was preferable. But the choice, as he saw it, was between the true church and a false one. The Catholic position was that the true church was the one founded in Rome by Peter and that, although reform was required within, it still remained the true and only church. Luther was brought up in that tradition and only broke with Rome reluctantly. Calvin, who came later, had evolved the idea of an elect, which made him look anew at what a church ought to be. Because of his ideas, he did not need to take the existing church into account and could build a system outside it. Knox came on the scene when this shift in thinking had taken place. He did not need to seek compromise with the Old Church or change within it. He had the option of an alternative church and made a fundamental choice to reject the Old Church. If it was not *the* church, then it must be a false church. The pope who headed it must therefore be an imposter since he denied that anyone outside the old system could gain salvation. The Roman Church was opposed to the truth and was therefore Antichrist. Given the choice between true and false churches, Knox's position was logical, just as the position of the papacy was logical in condemning him as a heretic.

From our more tolerant and relativist standpoint we can sympathise with Knox, but we find it difficult to identify with his absolute certainties. We are more inclined to ask why he chose the course of action he did. To answer that fully takes us behind all the ideological questions and actions of the characters in the story, to the character of Knox himself. The *personae* which Knox adopted of preacher, prophet, pastor, are the outward faces: what of the inner man? Some insight into that question can be gained from Knox's letters to his friends, in which he confesses his true feelings, and to political allies, in which a hidden agenda is revealed. The overall impression after reading a number of these is that Knox was a much nicer man than his public image. He shows sensitivity and humility – even self-doubt – which could not have been deduced from the public *persona*. He was also a very serious man. He possessed a sense of humour but it was of a heavy sort and we cannot ever imagine him giggling, or with a twinkle in his eye at some subtle joke. His letters, even the intimate ones to his women friends, tend to be dominated by theological issues. The preacher in him finds it difficult to stop preaching and although he seems superficially more like Luther than the more ascetic Calvin, his letters do not have the same amount of chatter and trivia about family life.

Although his home seems to have been happy, he must have imposed great strains upon it by his workaholic lifestyle. He was constantly travelling, and apart from brief periods of peace in Geneva from September 1557 to October 1558, and in Edinburgh in 1564, hardly a year passes in which he did not undertake a gruelling journey. No long journey was easy in those days and even if we allow for the fact that Knox was allowed the luxury of horses and the hospitality of wealthy Protestants, he toured Scotland, traversed England, and criss-crossed Europe, clocking up an astonishing mileage after he left the galleys in 1549. Undoubtedly this peripatetic activity helped him to widen the impact of his message and also to widen his personal horizon. But no matter how much Knox travelled he would always remain by temperament and inclination an outsider, that species of human who is never absorbed into the crowd but stands apart, critical and independent of mind.

He also remained a quintessential Lowland Scot. It has been said that while the cultural divide in England is north-south, in Scotland it is east-west and Knox's kind of protestantism appealed to the character of the east-coast Scot. While it is facile to generalise, the qualities which are held dear in the character of Scots from the eastern seaboard are those to be found in Knox. His plain-speaking nature and his unsophisticated temperament would certainly have appealed to people more impressed with decency than social rank, and who tend to value ideas for the use to which they can be put rather than for their intrinsic worth. His mindset was that of a chief engineer rather than captain of the ship, a self-employed craftsman rather than an employer or a labourer. This archetype, confirmed by his humble upbringing, inevitably found an echo in the north rather than the south of England, and when we assess his attachment to England (which he never lost) it is probably the northern part that he longed for most. It was there that he had his congregation and there he met the Bowes ladies who played such important roles in his life.

It must remain speculation, but the lack of mention of Knox's parents in his early life points to the likelihood that they died when he was young. The mother-figure of Mrs Bowes would then have supplied a deep-seated need in Knox and accounted for his unusually close attachment to her. His fondness for women's company may have been the result of a search for a feminine component in his psyche. Although Knox is intensely masculine in his outward *persona*, and shared the attitudes of his time which today would be called chauvinist, he does not exhibit an aggressive attitude to women. The arguments advanced in the First Blast are easily distinguishable from the sexually-twisted view of women advanced by many Catholic medieval theologians. Knox was concerned with the role of women as power figures and, as has already been pointed out, he quite happily modified these views when it was expedient to do so. The real thrust of the First Blast was not against women in general but one woman in particular. It was *ad feminam* rather than misogynist. When he found false feminine figures, he rejected them with a vehemence that points to there being some truth in his dependence upon a feminine archetype. The Virgin Mary and her church were regarded as a 'shadow' to be rejected, and likewise the two Queen Marys. Intriguing as it is to apply Freudian and Jungian ideas to Knox, his relationships with women were not as obsessional as his detractors would have us believe.

Although Knox can never be described as having a theology in the sense of Luther or Calvin, several important strands can be isolated in his thinking. Undoubtedly he was influenced in his early days by Lutheran material and through Wishart by the Swiss movement. He was then subjected to other influences during his time in England before coming under Calvin's patronage in Geneva. But he took his theology where he needed it and is by no means a clone of Calvin's, especially, as we have seen, in his attitude to rulers. Richard L. Greaves, the American historian, in his excellent analysis of Knox's thought, *Theology and Revolution in the Scottish Reformation* [USA, 1980], says:

> No label except 'reformed' accurately represents Knox's theological and ecclesiastic position. While recognising his debts to others it must be emphasised that he consciously selected views from these sources and discarded others. He was not a truly original thinker, but nor was Calvin . . . the theology he developed reflects not only the views of others but also his own experience, mind, integrity and conviction of the need for reformation . . . Like Calvin he was an eclectic thinker, but unlike Calvin he was not a systematic theologian . . . he was a man of action who left his imprint on the international scene. [p. 223]

What then was the core of Knox's beliefs? Primarily his reliance on the Bible as the single source of authority: he disliked words being incorporated into the liturgy of the church which were not originally to be found in the Bible. His use of the Bible in his preaching and writing shows him to be particularly fond of the Old Testament. Time and again he quotes from the Pentateuch, Isaiah, Jeremiah and the Psalms. But his use of Judges, 1 and 2 Samuel and 1 and 2 Kings is also significant. He took the situations he found there as allegories for the contemporary situation in which he found himself. This is not to say that he believed these situations had been foreseen by the biblical writer, but when he found an echo he shouted aloud and made it resound in the ears of his listeners. His favourite analogy for Mary of Guise and her daughter Queen Mary, was that of Jezebel, the Queen whose animosity to Naboth the vineyard-owner led her to conspire to have him murdered so that she could steal his land.

From the Old Testament he derived the idea of a sovereign God who controlled and ruled over all life. This God saved through his grace, supremely revealed in the life, death and resurrection of Jesus Christ. The way in which grace was communicated to humanity was by faith, rather than good works or ceremonies of the church. This led him to two conclusions. The first was that all works or ceremonies were man-made unless they were to be found in the Bible. This meant that the church was *necessary* as the institution to provide preaching and the sacraments (and Knox would have put them in that order of priority) but was not *essential* for salvation. Those who were saved, the elect, became such through the grace of God. Knox admitted that the reason why some were saved and others were not was a mystery, but ultimately one that remained closed to mere mortals. The decision belonged to God who was just. It is wrong to attribute to him strict ideas of predestination. In his own words election represented 'a plain difference betwixt one sort of man and another', the idea of opportunity and special responsibility. Or, as Eustace Percy puts it, 'There is no more necessary connection between divine election and personal salvation than there is between natural selection and individual expectation of life.' In other words he did not damn all those who were not of his view, since the church of the elect was an invisible body, visible only to God. His idea of sin was to rebel against God's will by failing to do good or failing to prevent evil. Thus it was always possible that the godly could fall from grace. He did not believe that the elect could do no wrong.

The second consequence, which flowed logically from this view, was that those who set up a system of salvation, by which someone was offered grace by the performance of a ceremony or by paying for an indulgence, were guilty not simply of fraud but idolatry. It was a false worship. Knox saw such practices as evil and this led him to condemn the Roman Catholic Church as Antichrist. Significantly he does not call individual Catholics evil, or Antichrist, but it is the system itself which is evil. That explains his vehemence against the mass in which the word 'sacrifice' is used (see pp.49ff). Knox's passionate beliefs on

Holy Communion had several consequences. They brought about an emphasis in the Scottish Reformed tradition which was anti-sacramental and suspicious of the least whiff of idolatry. Anything which hinted of the mass, such as candles and vestments, was repudiated vehemently. But there was a positive side. The reaction against kneeling for communion resulted in an alternative tradition in which the believers sat round a table and received communion in both bread and wine. Knox did not share with Calvin his desire for frequent communion but this resulted in its becoming a special and solemn occasion. Those who try to find in Knox (notably Eustace Percy) someone who had Holy Communion at the centre of his church are mistaken. For Knox, preaching was the prime activity of the minister.

In his preaching, however, we find surprisingly little of the New Testament. Indeed W. Croft Dickinson, the most recent editor of Knox's *History* [1949], remarks:

> Throughout his life, dedicated to 'Christ Jesus his Evangel' the spirit of Christ is absent in his public work. Never in public do we find an appreciation of the message of St Paul, 'Though I speak with the tongues of men and of angels, and have not charity, I am become as sounding brass, or a tinkling cymbal'. Only at rare moments in the quietude of the chamber is that spirit revealed.

That damning indictment is echoed by the famous Protestant preacher C. H. Spurgeon, who said, 'John Knox undoubtedly preached the gospel of love − it is a pity he did not preach it more lovingly.' That raises the question whether Knox was primarily a minister of the Christian gospel: can he perhaps be better classified as a nationalist leader or revolutionary who happened to operate within the church − state situation of his day?

Knox is not easily reclassified as a Scottish nationalist: first because he was not primarily interested in promoting Reformed religion in Scotland alone, and on a number of occasions passed up the opportunity to make Scotland his first priority; secondly because he consistently argued for a rapprochement with England before and after the Reformation (Scottish Nationalists are usually less keen on such ideas); and thirdly, although he speaks of the elect as a nation, he does not identify the elect *with* the nation. The idea of the covenant between God and his people is found in Knox (and often in the Bible), but what if the ruler was idolatrous, as he himself had occasion to experience? Where would that leave the nation? He therefore does not use the idea of subscribing to a covenant as a way of identifying the godly nation, in the way it was to be taken up by his descendants in 1638 when they rebelled against Charles I. Knox's elect is composed of all nations. Knox's European credentials should not be ignored simply because he shared the same 'thrawn' independence as many of his fellow-countrymen. His achievements and attitudes are European rather than confined to Scotland.

What then of the other description which could be applied to Knox – that of revolutionary. In many respects the Scottish Reformation was a revolution rather than a restructuring of religion, in that the seat of authority was shifted and replaced with another. Let us first hear from Knox himself about the intentions of the Reformers in 1559 on the eve of their 'revolution', when he wrote his preface to *History*, Book II:

> Lest that Satan by our long silence shall take occasion to blaspheme, and to slander us the Protestants of the Realm of Scotland, as that our [f]act tended to sedition and rebellion, than to reformation of manners and abuses in religion, we have thought expedient, so truly and briefly as we can to commit to writing the causes moving us (us, we say, a great part of the nobility and barons of the realm) to take the sword of just defence against those who most unjustly seek our destruction . . . (we) seek nothing but Christ Jesus his glorious Evangel to be preached; his holy sacraments to be truly administered; superstition, tyranny and idolatry to be suppressed in this realm; and finally the liberty of this our native country to remain free from the bondage and tyranny of strangers.

There are echoes in these words of the Magna Charta (1215) and the Declaration of Arbroath (1320); but the key phrase is 'the sword of just defence'. This is the kernel of Knox's doctrine and it marks out his unique contribution to Reformation history. As R. L. Greaves puts it, 'Ultimately Knox's theory of active resistance contributed to the ideological tradition that culminated in the American Revolution. In terms of both his life and his thought, he was one of the most influential men of his age' (p. 224).

Although Knox and the nobility and barons of the realm were on the same side, apparently fighting for the same end, the basis on which they did so was radically different. The nobility were concerned to replace the Queen, who had forfeited the right to divine approval, with another monarch who would meet with divine approval. Knox's monarch did not reign by divine appointment, but by divine permission. The difference was that as soon as the monarch stepped out of line, then the godly commonwealth had not only the right, but the duty to bring him or her into line. If the monarch's crime was sufficiently serious then he or she ought to be deposed or put to death. Knox's position struck at the basis on which the monarchy and nobility operated in sixteenth-century Europe. They inherited their power through blood-lines and were supported by a religious system which gave them divine rights. Even Luther and Calvin, as we have seen, continued to endorse the idea that this kind of monarchy had divine approval. Knox had got it into his head (and it was his own idea rather than one borrowed from his colleagues) that there was a just and godly right to depose the ungodly ruler. If this idea had been universally adopted it would have meant that the sovereigns of Europe were subject, as governments are today, to the wishes of their people.

The weakness of Knox's position was that when there arose competing ideas of what was godly, and where there was no universal religious authority like the papacy to adjudicate and/or depose monarchs, another method had to be found for the judgment of the godly to be expressed. Today we might call that method democracy but nothing resembling it existed in the sixteenth century in any sense we would recognise, and even if it had, Knox would have wanted to modify it, since he would not have believed that a simple majority of citizens could be guaranteed to express the will of God. That was the job of those who studied and informed themselves from the Scriptures. Thus Knox's system cannot be called democracy. It is more like 'theocracy'. But since it relied on the idea that a group had the right outside the legal and political structure to resist or depose a monarch, it is rightly called revolution.

One may ask why the Scottish nobles who joined forces with Knox did not see the fundamental contradiction between his position and theirs. The answer is that they had far too much in common to fall out about ideology. Their common cause made them allies and while the lords could not have achieved their Reformation without the Congregation, neither could the Congregation have achieved their revolution without the nobles. As soon as their aims were achieved, the nobles saw to it that it was to be a Reformation on their terms rather than a revolution.

The moment when this came into the open was the private session between the leading preachers and the nobles prior to the General Assembly of June 1564. It developed into a debate on the issue between Maitland of Lethington and Knox, and the latter gives it thirty pages at the end of Book IV of his *History*, which shows the importance that he attached to it. Knox and Lethington had never seen eye to eye and throughout the four books of the *History* Knox makes frequent references to the perfidious twists and turns which Scotland's Machiavelli performed during the events of 1555–66. Lethington, in his turn, does not attempt to hide his contempt for Knox. The key section of the argument between the two men is reproduced (slightly abridged) containing the nub of the disagreement between Knox and the nobility. Lethington begins by taxing Knox with being obsessed with the peripheral issue of the Queen's attendance at Mass:

Lethington: Your continual crying is – the Queen's idolatry, the Queen's mass will provoke God's vengeance.
Knox: I hear not queens and kings excepted, but all unfaithful are pronounced to stand in one rank, and to be in bondage to one tyrant the devil . . .
L   Where will ye find that any of the prophets did so entreat kings and queens, rulers or magistrates?

K   In more places than one. Ahab was a king and Jezebel
    was a queen, and yet what the prophet Elijah said to the
    one and to the other, I suppose ye be not ignorant?

L   That was not cried out before the people to make them
    odious to their subjects.

K   That it was whispered in their ear or in a corner, I read
    not. Both the people and the court understood well what
    the prophet had promised – that dogs shall lick the blood
    of Ahab . . .

L   They were singular motions of the spirit of God and
    appertain nothing to this our age.

K   Then had the Scripture far deceived me, for St Paul
    teaches me that whatsoever is written in the Holy
    Scriptures is written for our instruction . . .

L   How will ye prove that the person placed in authority may
    be resisted, seeing that the apostle says – he that resists,
    resisteth the ordinance of God?

K   I say that the power is not to be understood as the unjust
    commandment of men, but of the just power wherewith
    God has armed his magistrates to punish sin and maintain
    virtue. But if any man should take from the hand of a
    lawful judge a murderer . . . this same man resisteth
    God's ordinance because he stayed God's sword from
    striking . . . if men oppose themselves to the blind rage
    of princes they resist not God but the devil who abuses
    the sword of God.

L   I understand what ye mean and one part I will not
    oppose, but I doubt the other. For if the Queen were
    to command me to slay John Knox because she is
    offended at him, I would not obey her. But, if she would
    command others to do it, I cannot tell if I would be found
    to defend him.

K   My lord, if ye be persuaded of my innocence and if God
    has given you such a power as you might deliver me, and
    yet you allowed me to perish, in doing so ye should be
    criminal and guilty of my blood.

L   Prove that, and win the play! . . . [here the conversation
    drifts away from the point but Lethington brings it back
    by asking Knox if he intends to usurp the powers given

to rulers] will ye make subjects to control their princes and rulers?

K   And what harm should the commonwealth receive if the corrupt affections of ignorant rulers were moderated, and so bridled by the wisdom and discretion of godly subjects, that they should do no wrong nor violence to any man?

L   All this is not to the point, for we are reasoning that the Queen would become such an enemy to our religion that she should persecute it, which I am assured she never will. Our question is – whether we may suppress the Queen's mass, or whether her idolatry will be laid to our charge?

K   What ye may do by force I dispute not. But what ye ought to do by God's express commandment that I can tell. Idolatry ought not only to be suppressed but the idolater ought to die the death, unless that we will accuse God.

L   By whom is the idolater commanded to die?

K   By the people of God. Hear Israel, says the Lord, if it be agreed that idolatry is committed in any one city . . . the whole people shall arise and destroy that city, sparing none.

L   But there is no commandment given to the people to punish their king if he be an idolater.

K   I find no more privilege granted unto kings by God than unto the people, to offend God's majesty.

L   I grant. But yet the people may not be judges unto their king to punish him, albeit he be an idolater.

K   God is the universal Judge, as well unto the King as to the people; so that what his word commands to be punished in the one is not to be absolved in the other.

L   We agree in that, but the people may not execute God's judgment, but leave it unto himself who will either punish by death, by war, by imprisonment or by some other plagues.

K   I know the last part of your reason to be true. But the first – that the people may not execute God's judgment against their king, I am assured that ye have no more warrant than your own imagination.

L   Why say ye so? I have the judgments of the most famous

men within Europe, of such as ye yourself will confess both godly and learned.

At this juncture Lethington read out a litany of Luther, Calvin, Bucer and Melanchthon in support of his case, suggesting that Knox was not only mistaken in his view but out of tune with the leading Protestant figures in Europe, as indeed he was on this issue. Yet it remains the key issue of the Scottish Reformation and one which was never fully resolved. It still surfaces in debates about the right to self-determination by the Scottish people, and those who take Knox's side believe that a Claim of Right places sovereignty in the hands of the people rather than in the person of a ruler.

As far as the original debate went, Lethington probably won on points, since he had isolated Knox's stance as unrepresentative and succeeded in keeping Knox on the defensive. He cleverly undermined Knox's favourite tactic of applying biblical analogies to contemporary events by arguing that because an incident occurred in the Old Testament, it did not mean that it could be used to explain or parallel a contemporary event: 'We are not bound to imitate extraordinary examples, unless we have the like commandment and assurance,' he argued, with some plausibility. On the question of action to be taken against the mass, Knox's call for death for idolaters sounds barbarian and harsh. In his defence it has to be said that he only believed that this was an option after suitable opportunity for repentance and also after proper judicial process (a standard he sadly allowed to slip when assessing the morality of the Rizzio killing). The contemporary verdict would probably go to Lethington, but for one thing.

Lethington is on the attack and does not require to defend the hereditary system which transfers power through marriage, and which makes genes supreme rather than ability or moral virtue. When we examine the basis on which the power of the sixteenth-century monarchy is based, we see that it is the inheritance of an élite, underwritten by law. But applying the Knox critique, neither inheritance nor law guarantees virtue, since the black sheep or the unjust law can be made supreme. Both are human systems with human weaknesses and both are corruptible. That is where Lethington's case begins to look weaker.

Knox's alternative – the truth as revealed in Scripture or as interpreted by the godly – is also unappealing, since we immediately realise that there is more than one way to interpret Scripture and there are texts which apparently contradict one another. Would we trust a set of preachers to interpret it more justly than we would a set of priests or Ayatollahs, or a king, for that matter? Yet in our own century we have seen leaders rise whose tyranny was manifestly evil. If Hitler or Stalin had been removed before their policies of genocide had been completed, how many millions of lives might have been saved? If the death squads of Amin and Pol Pot had been deprived by assassination of a leader, would their countries not have been better off? Would the Gulf War have taken place if Saddam Hussein had been toppled as Iraq's leader? The twentieth century has seen too many tyrants and dictators, with even more totalitarian powers than the medieval monarchs, to brush aside as archaic Knox's moral imperative to remove the tyrannical ruler by violence. As a just solution it is extremely relevant in countries where human rights are being ground underfoot and there is no recourse to Parliament or the law courts. Knox may not be true to Christ's gospel of peace, but he is in the company of freedom fighters throughout the world.

Implicit within Knox's thinking on the monarchy is the idea that government does not belong properly to kings but to the people. He would have got little support for that political ideology in his own time, but most western societies have subsequently moved to agree that sovereignty does indeed lie with the people. Some countries retain monarchy as the symbol of that authority and most have a universal franchise. Knox's 'godly law' has become the humanitarian law, one which commands universal acceptance and which can be changed if it is perceived to bear unjustly upon the people. We may not share Knox's theology but he was on the side of the future, whereas Lethington was on the side of the past. Knox's notions of the accountability of rulers, of power residing in the people (albeit limited by him to the godly ones), and of the need to devise a social system which gave equal opportunity through education to all citizens, are profoundly humanitarian when compared with the system which they challenged. If we put aside his menacing rhetoric about idolatry and his obsession with Old Testament parallels and examine the goals which he set for his revolution, he is entitled to his place in history in a line which runs through the American, French and Russian revolutions – and he emerges with significantly less blood on his hands than the leaders of these revolutions.

Of course the difference is that the Scottish 'revolution' did not happen. It was diverted into a cul-de-sac, and Knox transformed into a figure of puritanical oppression. It has been his fate to be principally remembered as an iconoclast when he had hoped to be remembered as the architect of a new church in Scotland. The tragedy is Scotland's tragedy. He had devised a system well-suited to the needs of a country that was poor, torn by social inequality and lacking a tranquil climate. Scots eventually preferred to squander their dreams by putting their faith in monarchs who knew little of the Scottish people and less of real life. The posthumous romantic twaddle surrounding Mary Queen of Scots and Bonnie Prince Charlie have become the accepted version of history, and the tragic mistakes of the past mythologised, in preference to facing up to the harsh reality of being a nation within Europe. Energies which could have built a better nation were diverted once again into the struggle against the English enemy, and the successors of Knox who espoused the religion of the people grew harsher and more desperate than Knox had ever been. The history of the seventeenth and eighteenth centuries are squalid replays of the battle in which Knox fought, and lacks much of the idealism of the Reformation period. Once the sword of the Lord had been drawn from its scabbard it was not easily returned. It has been said that 'it was no part of Knox's teaching that there must be conflict between church and state but the claims he made on behalf of the church made that conflict inevitable' [J. H. S. Burleigh]. That seems almost to lay at Knox's door the follies of the future, when a more just assessment would be that the responsibility lies with those who rejected his vision of a godly commonwealth.

Another way of assessing his contribution would be to imagine what would have happened if events had turned out differently. It is an entirely speculative exercise, but what if . . . the Book of Discipline had been accepted? Then Scotland would have been transformed from a backward country on the northern fringe of Europe to an educationally superior nation, in which the church would have been a leading force. The feudal and feuding nobles would not have been able to hold back the tide of 'people power'.

What if . . . such a thing had happened and Scotland had become another Switzerland with government devolved on area cantons, each finding its own form of church – state compact? The view of Scotland from afar is that of a single nation; but ethnically, geographically and historically it is several nations. It would have been ideally suited to such a canton system in the absence of a single monarch. The Catholics in the north-east would have been one canton, the Highlands another; then Tayside and Fife, the Lothians, and the south-west. All have their own distinctive character and demography. Within the European community it may yet happen and the future seems to lie with ethnic regions rather than nation states. Scotland had the chance to practise such an experiment 450 years ago.

What if . . . the opposite had happened and there had been annexation of Scotland by England and a joint-Reformed religion had been forged? That hypothesis is easier, because such an attempt was indeed made in 1584 by James VI, son of Mary Queen of Scots and no lover of the memory of Knox. When he became James I of Great Britain in 1603 he attempted to impose an episcopal system which would inevitably have led to the Church of Scotland becoming a province of the Anglican Church and subject to the state, in the same way as the Church of England was (and is). James was thwarted by a neo-Knox, Andrew Melville, the father of presbyterianism. When James's son Charles I tried the same scheme he was thwarted by the Covenanters, who signed in their own blood rather than submit to an alien system of religion in which doctrine and polity were controlled by the state.

Although Knox had personally favoured closer alliance with English protestantism, the principles which had fired his vision of a church free from the domination of the aristocracy were the cornerstone of the cause taken up by his successors, to prevent assimilation of the kirk into the Church of England.

There is a terrible irony here, for if Knox had got his way, such a joint-British Church would have been hastened. Although he would have wanted a radical version of protestantism without prayer books and vestments, he was likely to have had as much success in achieving that as he had had against Cox and company in Frankfurt (see pp. 78ff); and their church had become the religious establishment in England. There is no possibility that under Elizabeth Knox would have been allowed the freedom in his pulpit which he enjoyed under Mary Queen of Scots. Perhaps he would have retired from controversy, like Goodman and Willock, and slipped into a quiet country parish in the north of England. As Alec Cheyne has remarked, 'Knox was gloriously inconsistent and opportunist' [SJT, 16.1], so who knows?

What if . . . John Knox had stayed in Geneva? The odds are that he would have been happy. He had the knack of finding trouble throughout his life without looking for it. The basic difference he had with Calvin over resistance to ungodly rulers might have come to the fore, and Knox would have been expelled. But he only developed the theory as a consequence of his conflicts in England and Scotland. With no adversary looming large in his life he would probably have been a little bored but a lot happier and would have become a small footnote in the history of the European Reformation. As it is he attained the status of a giant figure on the Reformation monument in Geneva, along with Calvin, Beza and Farel.

What if . . . John Knox had not existed at all? The Reformation in Scotland would probably still have happened. It would have happened later, more tentatively and would not have had the same character. The lack of leadership in Scotland was evident in 1555 when they had to turn to Knox, an exile in Switzerland who had been eight years out of the country, and one can imagine that a Reformed Church designed by Lord James Stewart and Lethington would have been considerably less dynamic in the demands it made of the ruling class than the church that Knox negotiated, despite its being less than he wanted. One of his legacies was that the clergy was driven through struggle and poverty into identifying with the problems of its people in the decade following the Reformation. That forged an attitude of mind which enabled the Church of Scotland to be able to claim that it was both an established church and a church of the people.

Without John Knox that church would have been the poorer and Scotland would have lost one of its archetypal and seminal figures. His character and achievements are similar to those of many of the Old Testament prophets who were thorns in the flesh of the rulers of Israel. His prose never reaches the heights of an Isaiah, but his preaching had as much impact in his own time as Jeremiah's had in his, and Knox's fearless honesty towards his Queen ranks with that of Nathan and John the Baptist towards their monarchs. The Old Testament prophets were not diviners of the future. They discerned the signs of the times. Knox's penchant for applying Old Testament prophecies to sixteenth-century situations is not evidence of powers of prediction on the part of himself or the prophets. It is his way of using the Bible to effect his own prophecies about the need for rulers to be accountable to their subjects. History has shown that there will always be a need to challenge the abuse of power by rulers. Knox stands in a long line of prophetic figures who stood against the rulers of their day. His mistake was not that he turned back to the biblical prophets for inspiration, but that he lived at a time when the world was still not ready to abandon the idea of the divine right of kings for the idea of the godly commonwealth. His prophecy was made for his own times but was only to be realised long after his death. John Knox got it right – his mistake was only that he did so two centuries ahead of his time.

Appendix

Will the real John Knox please stand up?

Originally 1505 had been accepted as the year in which Knox was born. This seems to have arisen from David Buchanan's 1644 *History of the Reformation in Scotland*, in which 1505 is given, and a probable misreading of a 5 as a 6 in Archbishop Spottiswood's *History of the Church of Scotland* (published in 1655 but written by Spottiswood prior to his death in 1639). In 1579 Sir Peter Young, tutor to James VI, stated that Knox had been fifty-nine at the time of his death on November 24 1572. Young supplied information to the Swiss Reformer Beza for his series of portraits of Reformation figures (*Icones*) which appeared in 1580, and this gives Knox's age as fifty-seven when he died. This could have been a printer's error, for there were others in the text, or else a correction supplied by those still living in Geneva who knew the Reformer's true age. It is sometimes argued that Knox's references to himself as decrepit nearer the end of his life are more commensurate with a man in his sixties. But the exhausting mental and physical life he led from 1545 onwards, including nineteen months as a galley slave, would be sufficient to have diminished his vitality and to account for his state of body and mind. He suffered a stroke in his final years and lived in an age when health and diet were less conducive to long life than in our own.

The true portrait of John Knox is no less illusive. Strangely no painting was ever made of him during his lifetime and a collection of books on Knox throughout the centuries would yield a variety of portraits none of which seems to be of the same man! The portrait which appears in the first edition of *Icones* is the most widely accepted likeness, since it is generally supposed to be the one painted from memory by Adrian Vaensoun seven years after Knox's death and sent by Young to Beza. But the 1581 French edition of *Icones* has a different portrait. This could also be the Vaensoun one, which possibly had not arrived in time for the 1580 edition (Young sent the portrait and letter on November 13 1579). This 1581 version also turned up in *Chalcographia Britannica* in 1620, where for the first time it was claimed to be William Tyndale and was then used as a basis for an oil painting of the Bible translator. Whichever of the *Icones* versions we choose to accept, the description of Knox by Sir Peter Young has never been disputed and is the basis of many of the subsequent portraits.

THE ROYAL HOUSES OF ENGLAND, FRANCE AND SCOTLAND IN THE LIFETIME OF JOHN KNOX

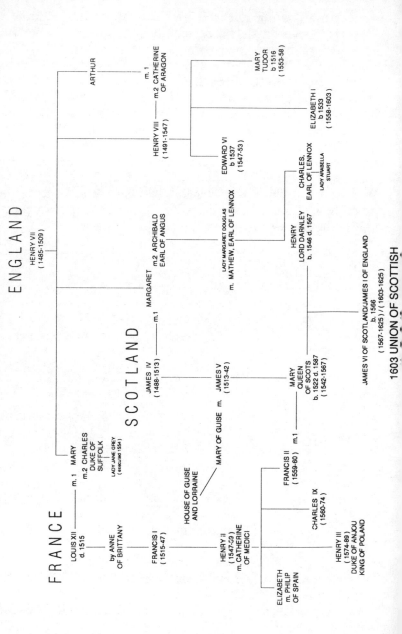

Select Bibliography

Dickinson, W.C. (ed.), *The History of the Reformation by John Knox*, 2 vols, London, Nelson, 1949.

Fraser, Antonia, *Mary Queen of Scots*, Mandarin, 1989.

Greaves, Richard L., *Theology and Revolution in the Scottish Reformation*, USA, Xion Univ Press, 1980.

Hazlett, Ian, *A Working Bibliography of Writings by John Knox*, Calviniana Vol X, pp 185–193, 1988.

Kyle, R.G., *The Mind of John Knox*, Ann Arbor, USA 1973.

Laing, David (ed.). *The Works of John Knox*, 6 vols, Edinburgh, Bannatyne Club 1846–64.

Lynch, Michael, *Edinburgh and the Reformation*, John Donald, 1981.

M'Crie, Thomas, *The Life of John Knox*, London, 1905.

McNeill, John T., *The History and Character of Calvinism*, Oxford, 1954.

Percy, Lord Eustace, *Life of Knox*, London, Hodder & Stoughton, 1937.

Reid, W. Stanford, *Trumpeter of God*, Grand Rapids, Baker Book House, USA 1982.

Ridley, Jasper, *John Knox*, Clarendon Press, 1968.

Shaw, Duncan (ed.), *John Knox Quartercentenary Papers*, St Andrew Press, 1975.

Watt, Hugh, *John Knox in Controversy*, Edinburgh, Nelson, 1950.

Index

196 INDEX